101 WAYS TO SAVE MONEY ON YOUR TAX

Legally!

101 WAYS TO SAVE MONEY ON YOUR TAX

Legally!

Updated for 2015–2016

ADRIAN RAFTERY

Wrightbooks
A Wiley Brand

This fifth edition published in 2015 by Wrightbooks
an imprint of John Wiley & Sons Australia, Ltd
42 McDougall St, Milton Qld 4064

Office also in Melbourne

First edition published by Wrightbooks in 2011. New edition published annually.

Typeset in 10.5/14 pt ITC Giovanni Std

© Adrian Raftery 2015

The moral rights of the author have been asserted

National Library of Australia Cataloguing-in-Publication data:

Creator:	Raftery, Adrian, 1971– author
Title:	101 Ways to Save Money on Your Tax — Legally!: 2015–2016 edition / Adrian Raftery.
Edition:	5th edition.
ISBN:	9780730320760 (pbk.)
	9780730320777 (ebook)
Notes:	Includes index.
Subjects:	Tax deductions — Australia.
	Taxation — Australia.
	Finance, Personal.
Dewey Number:	336.2060994

Cover design: Wiley

Cover and internal image: © cogal/iStockphoto.com

Tables 1.1, 1.2, 1.3, 1.4, 2.1, 2.2, 2.3, 2.4, 3.1, 3.2, 3.3, 4.2, 5.1, 6.1, 6.2, 8.1, 8.2, 8.3 © Australian Taxation Office for the Commonwealth of Australia.

Printed in Australia by Ligare Book Printer

10 9 8 7 6 5 4 3 2 1

Disclaimer

The material in this publication is of the nature of general comment only, and does not represent professional advice. It is not intended to provide specific guidance for particular circumstances and it should not be relied on as the basis for any decision to take action or not take action on any matter which it covers. Readers should obtain professional advice where appropriate, before making any such decision. To the maximum extent permitted by law, the author and publisher disclaim all responsibility and liability to any person, arising directly or indirectly from any person taking or not taking action based on the information in this publication.

Dedicated to the Irish cricket team who provided so much entertainment during the 2015 Cricket World Cup. May you be rewarded with Test match status in the near future.

Contents

About the author

Adrian Raftery (PhD, MBA, B Bus, FCA, CFP, F Fin, CTA, MAICD), aka Mr Taxman, is fast becoming one of Australia's leading commentators on all matters relating to tax and finance. With regular columns in various investment magazines, a senior lecturer position at Deakin University and frequent appearances on TV and in the media, Adrian is Australia's newest financial expert.

Part of Adrian's 'tax' appeal as a financial media commentator is due to his personable and approachable style. Just as importantly, Adrian's 25 years' experience as an award-winning accountant working with small and medium businesses, and as a personal tax expert, means he has the relevant knowledge and experience to give qualified advice.

Adrian is considered so good at what he does that he is one of the youngest Australian accountants to have advanced to

Fellowship with the Institute of Chartered Accountants at the age of 33 and had an award-winning Sydney accountancy firm at just 25! Adrian is also one of the country's leading experts on the rapidly growing Australian superannuation industry as he completed a PhD on self managed superannuation funds last year. These factors and Adrian's ability to translate complicated tax, superannuation and finance jargon into understandable and workable solutions are probably why 'Mr Taxman' is frequently called upon for his viewpoints by the Australian media.

How to use this book

This book is designed to be of benefit to 99.9 per cent of taxpayers. If you have an investment property, own a share portfolio, have money in superannuation, have a family, work as an employee or run your own business, there will be something in here for you.

While it is extremely unlikely that all 101 tips will be applicable to you, your family or your business, just feel comfortable knowing that one tip alone will be more than enough to pay for the investment you make in buying this book. This book has been written to take into account all phases of life, so if you find that only a few tips apply to you right now, don't worry because more tips will become relevant as you grow older. Make sure that you consult your own adviser to assess your own particular needs before implementing any of these tips.

If there is one constant with tax, it is change. That is why I update this book every year to take into account the latest federal budget changes in May. If you intend to use this book as a reference guide over a number of years, you should always check the latest tax legislation for the current figures and thresholds.

Remember that tax planning should be a year-round exercise, not merely one that's done in the last few weeks before 30 June. A lot of these strategies are just as useful on 1 July as they are on 30 June.

 Tip

When you see this box throughout the book, it will provide you with a handy suggestion in relation to the particular money-saving strategy.

Tax fact

When you see this box throughout the book, it will provide you with an interesting fact.

Pitfall

When you see this box throughout the book, it will outline a potential pitfall in relation to this money-saving strategy that you need to look out for.

Bonus resources

When you see this box throughout the book, it will provide you with a tool or a calculator available on my website www.mrtaxman.com.au to help explain or work out a strategy.

FAQ

When you see this box throughout the book, it will provide you with an answer to a frequently asked question that I have received from readers of previous editions of this book.

Proposed change

When you see this box throughout the book, it will outline a tax change which has been proposed by the government but has not been put through as legislation as at date of publication. Before making any decisions, ensure that you check the status of these proposed changes as there may be variations to the original proposal as it passes through both houses of parliament.

Introduction

Three years ago, my wife and I were extremely fortunate to celebrate the birth of our son Hamish via a friend who acted as a surrogate mum. Before we started the surrogacy process, I remember her telling us that she had a gift to bear children, but 'a gift is not a gift unless it is given'.

I feel the same way about this book. Ever since I started working as an accountant at the age of 18, I have had a gift (some would say it is a curse) for understanding tax. But as a gift should be given, I have decided to share some great tax tips with you for a small tax-deductible fee (that is, the price of this very cheap book!).

This book has two objectives. First, I would like to help maximise everyone's refunds by making you more aware of the different ways that are available to help you save money on your tax legally. Second, through the setting of boundaries, I wish to reduce the amount of fraudulent claims made so that we all pay a fairer share of tax.

My motivation for writing this book was the number of families out there who didn't understand all the different types of government benefits and tax concessions that were available to them. I hope that this book will help reduce the confusion and that you will start claiming more of what you are legally entitled to.

This book is split into various parts in line with some key areas surrounding your finances:

▶ you and your family

▶ your employment

▶ your education

▶ your investment properties

▶ your shares

▶ your superannuation

▶ your business.

In each part I will share with you a number of tips and strategies that you can implement to save money on your taxes — legally!

You should leave no stone unturned in your quest to legally minimise your tax. While everyone should pay their fair share of tax, Kerry Packer summed it up best when he famously said 'don't tip them!'

Now I don't expect that every single tip will be applicable to every single person out there but I am confident that there will be at least one tip that will save you more than the cost of this book. Some tips will maximise your refund, others will minimise your tax, while others will simply save you money. Some may save you millions over a lifetime, others just a few dollars. But times are tough and every dollar counts.

Whatever you get out of this book, I hope it is positive and not too taxing! And this is my gift to you.

Mr Taxman

Part I

You and your family

From marriage and children right through to divorce, retirement and ultimately death, all families encounter many life-changing events. And in nearly all of these events, there are tax consequences along the way.

The Australian tax system offers a range of tax benefits including credits, refunds, offsets and bonuses to support families. Some people feel ambivalent about putting their hand out for government entitlements. But don't be shy in claiming your fair share. After all, the government doesn't get shy when it comes to taxing you!

Tax fact

Tax evasion and tax avoidance are *illegal* ways of reducing your tax payable. Tax planning and tax minimisation are *legal* ways of reducing your tax payable.

Part I looks at the tax concessions available to families, the special considerations you need to look out for, as well as some simple strategies to save tax within your family.

 Tip

You need a tax file number (TFN) to be eligible for any of these tax concessions, as do your spouse and your children if they have income, superannuation or investments.

1 *Marriage*

Accountants are frequently asked two questions by couples who are just about to get married: 'Are there are any tax implications once we tie the knot?' and 'Do we need to start doing joint tax returns?'

Your wedding day is a special day. So I'm perplexed as to why on earth the bride and groom are thinking about the ATO during such an exciting time in their lives!

You don't need to worry about tax in the lead-up to your nuptials. Unless you are involved in a business together, you don't have to lodge a combined tax return. Any share of joint investments, such as interest, dividends and rental properties, is still recorded separately in your respective tax returns.

 Tip

You don't have to lodge a combined tax return if you're married. Any joint income is recorded separately in your respective tax returns.

You do need to show on your return that you now have a spouse, and disclose his or her taxable income each year.

Pitfall

The combined income of married couples is taken into account if you don't have private health insurance (an extra 1 per cent Medicare levy is charged if you earn over $180 000 combined, increasing to 1.5 per cent for couples earning more than $280 000) as well as when calculating Family Assistance Office benefits such as child care rebates and family tax benefits.

If you elect to change your name, you can notify the tax office simply by noting it on the front cover of your next return. You don't need to provide any certified documents.

According to the ATO, the definition of spouse has been extended so that both de facto relationships and registered relationships are now recognised. Your 'spouse' is another person (whether of the same sex or opposite sex) who:

▶ is in a relationship with you and is registered under a prescribed state or territory law

▶ although not legally married to you, lives with you on a genuine domestic basis in a relationship as a couple.

Tax fact

Since 1 July 2009, people living in same-sex relationships have been treated in the same way as heterosexual couples for tax purposes. The ATO has outlined some of the tax concessions now open to same-sex couples, including:
▶ Medicare levy reduction or exemption
▶ Medicare levy surcharge

(continued)

Tax fact *(cont'd)*

- ► net medical expenses tax offset
- ► dependant tax offset
- ► pensioner tax offset
- ► SchoolKids Bonus
- ► spouse super contributions tax offset
- ► main residence exemption for capital gains tax.

It is not unusual to find a couple where each owns a main residence that was acquired before they met. However, spouses are only entitled to one main residence exemption for capital gains tax (CGT) purposes between them. If both members of a couple own a main residence they must do either of the following:

- ► select one residence for the exemption
- ► apportion the CGT exemption between the two residences.

Provided the homes meet the requirements for the main residence exemption, they will both be wholly exempt from CGT for the period prior to the couple being treated as spouses. However, from the time the couple became spouses, only one exemption is available, though this may be divided between the two dwellings.

Example

Mary bought a house in 1992. She lived in it right up to the day she married Matthew in 2006 and moved into his house, which he had purchased in 2000. As they elected to treat Matthew's house as their main residence, Mary will be subject to CGT on her house from 2006. She will not be liable for CGT on any capital growth in the 14 years prior to becoming Matthew's spouse.

2 Income splitting

Income splitting is a legitimate tax-planning tool and one of the easiest strategies to implement. There are a few simple strategies for you to follow and they all mainly revolve around the marginal tax rates for yourself and your spouse, both now and in the future. The tax rates for individuals, not including the Medicare and other levies, are shown in table 1.1.

The goal is to try to level the income of couples so that they are paying tax at the same marginal rate. While income from personal exertion (such as your salary) cannot be transferred to the other partner, there is scope to have passive income from investments transferred if the assets are held in the lower-earning spouse's name.

Table 1.1: tax rates for individuals excluding levies (2015–16)

Taxable income	Tax on this income
0–$18 200	Nil
$18 201–$37 000	19c for each $1 over $18 200
$37 001–$80 000	$3572 plus 32.5c for each $1 over $37 000
$80 001–$180 000	$17 547 plus 37c for each $1 over $80 000
$180 001 and over	$54 547 plus 45c for each $1 over $180 000

Source: © Australian Taxation Office for the Commonwealth of Australia.

It amazes me how many smart business people are really dumb when it comes to reducing tax. Too often I see rich business people paying the highest tax rate (49 per cent) on interest or dividend income while their spouses don't fully use their $18 200 tax-free threshold.

Tip

Ensure that all investments are in the name of the lower-earning spouse so that they can take advantage of the lower tax rates (particularly the first $18 200, which is tax-free) on any investment income derived. Likewise, have all passive deductions, such as charitable donations, in the higher-earning spouse's name as they may get a return of up to 49 per cent, depending on their income level.

The best tax outcome can be achieved with a low-income earner holding investment assets. They could earn up to $20 542 tax-free (see p. 18), receive a refund of all imputation credits and pay less tax on capital gains.

Example

If an investor on the top marginal tax rate of 49 per cent had a $100 000 capital gain they would pay $24 500 in tax and Medicare levy. If an investor with no other income had a $100 000 capital gain they would pay $8547—a saving of $15 953.

 Pitfall

Any tax benefit derived by transferring an income-producing asset from one spouse to another may be lost if there is CGT to pay on assets originally acquired after 19 September 1985.

If you transfer an income-producing asset to your spouse you may need to find out the market value of the asset from a professional valuer. This is regardless of what you actually receive because the transaction is not independent nor is it at arm's length. In this situation either party could exercise influence or control over the other in connection with the transaction.

 Tip

If you do not have a spouse, or you are both in the highest tax brackets, consider creating an investment company that is taxed at a flat rate of 30 per cent (proposed to decrease to 28.5 per cent for small companies from 1 July 2015) for all income.

---

3 Dependant (invalid and carer) tax offset

The dependant (invalid and carer) tax offset (DICTO) is only available to taxpayers who maintain a dependant who is genuinely unable to work due to carer obligation or disability.

Tax fact

The DICTO has consolidated the following tax offsets:

- ▶ invalid spouse
- ▶ carer spouse
- ▶ housekeeper
- ▶ housekeeper (with child)
- ▶ child housekeeper
- ▶ child housekeeper (with child)
- ▶ invalid relative
- ▶ parent/parent-in-law.

(continued)

Tax fact *(cont'd)*

The ATO may deem you eligible for the DICTO if the following applies:

▶ you contribute to the maintenance of your spouse, your parent (or your parent's spouse), your child (aged 16 or over) or siblings (aged 16 or over)

▶ your dependant was being paid either:

☐ a disability support, a special needs disability support or an invalidity service pension

☐ a carer allowance for a child or sibling aged 16 or over

☐ your combined adjusted taxable income as a couple was $150 000 or less

☐ your dependant's adjusted taxable income was less than $10 422

☐ you and your dependant were Australian residents (not just visiting).

If you satisfy the above and your dependant's adjusted taxable income was $285 or less and you maintained him or her for the whole year, you can claim the maximum dependant (invalid and carer) tax offset of $2535.

 Pitfall

The DICTO is reduced by $1 for every $4 that your dependant's adjusted taxable income exceeds $282.

 Tip

You may be able to receive more than one amount of DICTO if you contributed to the maintenance of more than one dependant during the year, including if you had different spouses during the year.

Proposed change

It was announced in the 2014–15 federal budget that the government would abolish the dependent spouse tax offset from 1 July 2014. However, at date of publication the proposed change was not yet law, so it may be possible to claim this offset (of up to $2471) in your 2014/15 income tax return if your adjusted taxable income was $150 000 or less; your spouse's adjusted taxable income was less than $10 166; your spouse was born before 1 July 1952 and neither of you are eligible for Family Tax Benefit Part B.

Tax fact

The ATO defines your 'adjusted taxable income' as the sum of the following amounts, less any child support that you have paid:

▶ taxable income
▶ adjusted fringe benefits (reportable fringe benefits × 0.53)
▶ tax-free pensions or benefits
▶ income from overseas not reported in your tax return
▶ reportable super contributions
▶ total net investment loss for both financial investments and rental properties.

Example

Marlene and Saxon are married. Marlene is genuinely unable to work and has no salary or wage income. They have rental properties and a share portfolio. Saxon has also entered into a salary-sacrificing arrangement to boost his super. His taxable income is $130 000 after claiming a total net investment loss of $18 000. He has reportable super contributions of $17 000.

(continued)

Example *(cont'd)*

Saxon's adjusted taxable income is $165 000 ($130 000 + $18 000 + $17 000). As Saxon's adjusted taxable income is over the income threshold for this offset ($150 000) he is not eligible to claim the dependant (invalid and carer) tax offset.

4 *Children*

Any income that has been earned by your child's efforts, such as wages from an after-school job, is considered 'excepted income' and is taxed at the general adult tax rates regardless of whether your child is under 18. However, you should be cautious when putting investments in your child's name because minors do not enjoy the same tax-free thresholds as adults on this type of income, known as 'eligible income'. Table 1.2 sets out the tax rates that apply to minors' eligible income.

Table 1.2: tax on eligible income for minors (2015–16)

Taxable income	Tax on this income
$0–$416	Nil
$416–$1307	66c for each $1 over $416
$1307 and over	45% of total income

Source: © Australian Taxation Office for the Commonwealth of Australia.

 Pitfall

Minors under the age of 18 are taxed at the highest marginal tax rate for 'eligible income' (such as interest, dividends and trust distributions) over $416 per annum.

If some of your child's income is excepted income and the rest is eligible income, he or she will pay ordinary rates on the excepted income and pay at the higher rate on the eligible income.

Example

Louie is 17 on 30 June. He earned $8780 from a part-time job. He also received $920 in interest from money he had saved over the years from gifts. Therefore, he has an excepted income of $8780 and is entitled to the tax-free threshold of $18 200 for this income. He also has eligible income of $920 interest, which is taxed at the special higher rates.

A child is eligible from birth for a TFN from the ATO. If your child does not supply their TFN to the bank or share registry, then 47 per cent tax will be withheld on interest earnings over a threshold of $420 as well as on all unfranked dividends.

Children do not need to lodge a tax return if their assessable income is less than $416. However, if tax has been withheld from them by an investment body or employer, then they must lodge a return in order to get that money returned to them.

 Tip

If you have an adult child who has a job while going to university or TAFE then he or she may be able to claim a deduction for certain expenses if there is a sufficient connection between their course and their assessable income. Some expenses that they might be able to claim in this instance include:

▶ depreciation of assets (such as computers, desks and bookshelves) used for studying purposes
▶ journals and periodicals
▶ photocopying and printing costs

(continued)

Tip *(cont'd)*

▶ stationery

▶ student union fees

▶ textbooks

▶ travel from work to place of study.

They wouldn't be entitled to a deduction for any tuition fees payable under HELP or any repayments of outstanding HELP debts.

Earnings from a child's investments must be declared by the person who rightfully owns and controls the investment, not the person whose name it is in, or whose name it is held in trust for. This is regardless of whether the money is spent on resources for the child.

Example

Sarah opens an account for her three-year-old daughter, Samantha, by depositing $8000. Sarah is signatory to the account and she also makes regular deposits and withdrawals to pay for Samantha's preschool expenses. The ATO would deem that the money belongs to Sarah and any interest earned from this account must be declared for tax by her.

If the funds in the account are made up of money received as birthday or Christmas presents, pocket money or savings from part-time earnings such as newspaper rounds, and these funds are not used by any person other than the child, then the interest earned is the child's income.

 Pitfall

Children are not eligible for the low-income tax offset against unearned income, such as interest. The rebate can only be offset against excepted income.

5 *Paid parental leave*

Eligible working parents of children born or adopted after 1 January 2011 may be entitled to the paid parental leave scheme to help them care for a new baby. The pay is for up to 18 weeks at the national minimum wage (currently $641.05 per week before tax) and is paid by either your employer or the government (where employers do not provide parental leave entitlements). You can claim for paid parental leave up to three months in advance.

To be eligible you must have worked at least 330 hours across 10 of the 13 months prior to the birth of your child, but your annual salary must also be less than $150 000. The work test has been extended so that mothers can count periods of paid parental leave they've taken for earlier births as 'work'.

Tax fact

Paid parental leave is subject to income tax and may also affect other government benefits such as child support, health care cards, public housing and dependent spouse rebates. In contrast, the Newborn Upfront Payment and Supplement is not taxable and not considered income for family assistance or social security purposes. For more information on paid parental leave go to www.australia.gov .au/paidparentalleave.

Parents are also eligible for the Maternity Immunisation Allowance, which is one of the few benefits that is not means tested. The allowance is paid in two instalments — one prior to your child's second birthday and the second before they turn five.

Tax fact

For children born after 1 March 2014, Family Tax Benefit Part A recipients may be entitled to a $514 Newborn Upfront Payment and up to $1542.45 for a Newborn Supplement (reduced to $1028.15 in total for subsequent children), payable via normal fortnightly payments over a three-month period. These payments are not taxable.

6   *Dad and partner pay*

To help partners bond with their new baby, eligible working partners of children born or adopted after 1 January 2013 may be entitled to a single 'dad and partner pay'. It is a one-off payment of up to two weeks at the national minimum wage (currently $641.05 per week before tax).

To be eligible you must have worked at least 330 hours across 10 of the 13 months prior to the birth of your child, but your annual salary must also be less than $150 000. You can be eligible if you work full time, part time, casually, seasonally, on contract or in a family business. You cannot be working or receiving paid leave during the period of claiming the dad and partner pay.

 Tip

In addition to dad and partner pay, families may be eligible for other family assistance such as paid parental leave and the Family Tax Benefit.

Claims must be lodged by the partner who is eligible to receive the payment. You can claim the dad and partner pay up to three months in advance or within a year following your child's birth or adoption. Employers are not required to pay this entitlement as it is solely administered and paid by the Department of Human Services.

Child care

Ask the parents of any young child and they will tell you that their biggest expense is child care. If you have a child who is attending child care services approved by, or registered with, the government you may be eligible for the Child Care Benefit (CCB). You can apply for the benefit at the Family Assistance Office. The amount you receive will depend on the type and amount of care that you use, your income, the reason you are using care and the number of children that you have in care.

> ☼ **Tip**
>
> If you have identified that you were eligible for the CCB in previous financial years, but have not received it, you can lodge a lump-sum claim with the Family Assistance Office. You must do this within two years of the end of the financial year for which you are claiming.

The Child Care Rebate is additional help available to eligible working families to assist with covering the cost of child care. It is a 50 per cent rebate, up to $7500 per child per year per primary claimant, based on the out-of-pocket cost for approved child care after the CCB has been paid. The maximum amount of \$7500 is frozen (that is, not indexed) until 30 June 2017. Note that the Child Care Rebate is a different payment from the CCB. To receive the rebate you must first claim the CCB for approved care.

Tax fact

According to the ATO, you may be eligible to claim the Child Care Rebate if you:

▶ were eligible for the CCB, even if you received no payment because your income was too high
▶ passed the work/training/study test
▶ used approved child care such as long day care, family day care, in-home care, outside school hours care, vacation care and/or some occasional care services.

Parents can claim up to 50 hours of CCB per child per week dependent on passing a work/training/study test. Once eligible, the rebate is paid weekly or fortnightly by Centrelink based on child care attendance information it receives electronically from your service provider. Even if your child is absent from child care, the CCB and Child Care Rebate can still be paid in some situations. You can receive payments for up to 42 absences per financial year, if you are charged for child care. These absent days can be taken for any reason with no evidence required.

Proposed change

It was announced in the 2015–16 federal budget that the CCB and Child Care Rebate would be abolished on 1 July 2017 and replaced with the Child Care Subsidy (CCS). Up to 100 hours of care per child per fortnight will be subsidised, dependent on a new work activity

Proposed change *(cont'd)*

test. Families with incomes under $65000 will receive a CCS of 85 per cent, reducing to 50 per cent for those families with incomes over $170000. A cap of $10000 will be applied to families with incomes over $185000.

Low-income earners

There are a few tax benefits available if you are a low-income earner, such as when you work part time.

Low-income tax offset

The low-income tax offset (LITO) is a tax rebate for individuals on lower incomes. In 2015–16, the LITO will provide a tax rebate of $445 for individuals who earn less than $37000. The offset is reduced by 1.5 cents for every dollar that your taxable income exceeds $37000, before eroding entirely at $66667.

 Tip

Low-income earners can effectively earn up to $20542 each year tax-free. So if you have a spouse who is not working, consider an income-splitting strategy to save as much as $10065 in tax.

To be eligible for LITO, you must be a resident for tax purposes and lodge a tax return. The ATO will automatically apply this offset to your assessment for you if you're entitled to it.

Pitfall

Minors cannot use the LITO to reduce tax payable on their unearned income.

Bonus resources

Go to my website www.mrtaxman.com.au for a low-income tax offset calculator to work out the amount of offset you are entitled to.

Superannuation co-contribution

If your total income is under the low-income threshold of $35 454 and you contribute $1000 post-tax to your super fund, the government will match it by 50 per cent with a further $500. The super co-contribution gradually phases out to nil (by 3.333 cents per dollar) at the higher income threshold of $50 454.

Superannuation spouse contribution tax offset

You are entitled to a rebate of up to $540 if you make contributions into your spouse's superannuation fund, if your spouse's assessable income and reportable fringe benefits are less than $13 800.

The rebate is 18 per cent of the lesser of:

▶ $3000 reduced by $1 for every dollar that your spouse's assessable income and reportable fringe benefits exceed $10 800

▶ the total of the eligible spouse contribution.

> **! Tax fact**
>
> The ATO outlines that tax offsets and tax deductions are not the same. Tax offsets are taken directly off your tax, while tax deductions are taken off your assessable income, which is used to calculate your tax. So each $1 of tax offset means you pay $1 less tax, regardless of your taxable income.

Low-income superannuation contribution

The government currently contributes up to $500 annually into the superannuation account of workers on adjusted taxable incomes of up to $37 000 to ensure that no tax is paid on superannuation guarantee contributions.

> **📢 Proposed change**
>
> The low-income superannuation contribution has been repealed but will continue to be payable in respect of concessional contributions made up to and including the 2016–17 year.

9 *Senior and pensioner tax offset*

Senior Australians or pensioners may be eligible for an offset that allows them to earn more income before they have to pay tax and the Medicare levy.

As we saw earlier, if you are under the pension age (currently 65 but proposed to increase to 67 in 2023 and 70 by 2035), you can earn an income of up to $20 542 before any tax is payable (see p. 17).

The tax rules get even better when you reach age pension age (or service pension age), as you may be able to access more generous tax-free thresholds, known as the senior and pensioner tax offset (SAPTO). Table 1.3 shows the thresholds for the SAPTO.

Table 1.3: thresholds for senior and pensioner tax offsets (SAPTO) (2015–16)

	Maximum offset	Shaded-out threshold (taxable income)*	Cut-out threshold (taxable income)
Single	$2 230	$33 044	$50 884
Couple (each)	$1 602	$29 739**	$42 555**
Couple (combined)	$3 204	$59 478	$85 110
Couple (separated by illness)	$4 080	$64 088	$96 728

* Maximum offset reduced by 12.5 cents for each $1 in excess of shaded-out threshold.
** A taxpayer's taxable income is taken to be half the couple's combined taxable income.
Source: © Australian Taxation Office for the Commonwealth of Australia.

Tip

Senior Australians are not required to pay any income tax if their income is below $33 044 for singles (or $29 739 each for couples). But if senior Australians derive income from a share portfolio they are encouraged to lodge a tax return, as they will receive a nice refund from all of the excess franking credits attached to their dividends.

Tax fact

If you're single, you can earn up to $33 044 (and $29 739 each for couples) in non-super income without paying a cent of tax because of the application of SAPTO and LITO. Any additional superannuation benefit that you receive from a taxed source is tax-free.

Bonus resources

Go to my website www.mrtaxman.com.au for a calculator to estimate the senior and pensioner tax offset.

Tax fact

Since 1 July 2014, senior Australian homeowners who have owned their family home for at least 25 years and who decide to downsize will have the option to invest surplus funds (up to $200 000) in a savings account that will be exempt from the age pension means test for up to 10 years.

Tax fact

Since 1 July 2014, the mature age worker tax offset is no longer available after it was abolished in the 2014/15 federal budget.

10 Other government benefits

There are so many different types of government benefits these days that it is no wonder some families are confused, and aren't claiming everything that they should be entitled to. Most entitlements are means tested, which means the benefits you receive are reduced as your income increases.

Tip

If you're in doubt when estimating your annual income, it is always better to overestimate. It can be difficult to repay a debt to Centrelink if you have already spent the cash!

Family Tax Benefit Part A

This benefit helps with the cost of raising dependent children and dependent full-time students under the age of 18. The amount of the benefit is determined by your family income as well as the number and age of your dependants. It will only be paid up to the end of the calendar year that your teenager is completing school.

Family Tax Benefit Part B

Restricted to families where the primary earner has an adjusted taxable income under $150 000, this benefit provides extra assistance to families with one main income. The lower-earning parent can earn up to $5329 per annum before the benefit reduces.

 Proposed change

From 1 July 2015, the Family Tax Benefit Part B payments will be limited to families whose youngest child is under six years of age.

SchoolKids Bonus

Eligible families receiving Family Tax Benefit A , with an annual adjusted taxable income under $100 000, are automatically entitled to a SchoolKids Bonus payment of $211 for each primary school student and $421 for each secondary school student every six months (paid in January and July each year).

> **Tax fact**
>
> The SchoolKids Bonus has been abolished with the last instalment to be paid in July 2016.

Parenting payment

This payment provides financial help for people who are the primary carers of children. It is means tested on both your income and assets.

Better start for children with a disability

Families with children under the age of seven that have been diagnosed with sight or hearing impairments, cerebral palsy, Down syndrome, fragile X syndrome, Prader Willi syndrome, Williams syndrome, Angelman syndrome, Kabuki syndrome, Smith-Magenis syndrome, CHARGE syndrome, Cornelia de Lange syndrome, Cri du Chat syndrome or microcephaly (before their sixth birthday) are eligible for funding towards early intervention.

The $12 000 early intervention funding (capped at $6000 per annum) is paid to service providers on a fee-for-services basis via the Department of Families, Housing, Community Services and Indigenous Affairs (FaHCSIA).

First home saver account

First home saver accounts (FHSA) are available for those aged between 18 and 65 as a way to save for your first home through a combination of government contributions and low taxes. The government will contribute an extra 17 per cent to your savings into your FHSA, up to $1020 each year (that is, a maximum contribution threshold of $6000). Savings are taxed at only 15 per cent. No further contributions can be made once the balance reaches the account cap of $90 000.

 Proposed change

It was announced in the 2014–15 federal budget that the FHSA scheme will be abolished from 1 July 2015 with account holders being able to withdraw their balances without restriction at that date. While existing account holders will continue to receive the government co-contribution (and all associated tax and social security concessions) for the 2013–14 income year, new accounts opened from 13 May 2014 will not be eligible for any concessions.

The following additional benefits may also be available to families:

▶ large family supplement (ceasing 1 July 2016)

▶ multiple birth allowance

▶ rent assistance

▶ health care card.

 Pitfall

Under the gifting rules, the maximum amount that you can gift to a friend or relative is $10 000 in each financial year and $30 000 in total over the previous five-year period. Any excess amounts are added back as part of your assets under the assets test.

11 *Family breakdown*

While we all want to have the perfect marriage and live happily ever after, the sad reality is that approximately one-third of marriages end in divorce in Australia.

The tax system has provisions in place to assist with easing the financial burden of separating families. These provisions apply to capital gains tax, superannuation and income from child- and partner-support payments.

Transfer of assets

Normally, when you sell an asset that was acquired after 19 September 1985, you are liable for CGT. However, when you transfer assets to your spouse as a result of the breakdown of your relationship, it is classified as an 'automatic rollover' of those assets and you will not have to pay capital gains tax at that time. Any subsequent disposal of the asset will trigger the CGT provisions, except for the family home, which is exempt.

Tax fact

There is no CGT if you transfer a property to your former spouse under a court order following the breakdown of your marriage.

This rollover ensures the spouse who gives the assets disregards a capital gain or capital loss that would otherwise arise, and the one who receives the asset (the transferee spouse) will make the capital gain or capital loss when they subsequently dispose of the asset.

Pitfall

If you and your spouse divide your property under a private or informal agreement (not because of a court order, a binding financial agreement, an arbitral award or another agreement or award), marriage or relationship breakdown rollover does not apply.

Transfer of superannuation

The splitting of superannuation between divorcing partners is similarly treated as a rollover. As the funds are not being released as a payment, this rollover split does not need to wait until retirement.

Child support and spouse support payments

You do not need to include any child support or spouse support payments that you may receive in your taxable income, but they are part of your adjusted taxable income calculation for tax offset purposes. Similarly, there is no tax deduction available for child support or spouse support payments.

The ATO cooperates with the Child Support Agency to:

▶ supply information to the Child Support Agency for the purpose of calculating child support payments

▶ encourage lodgement of outstanding tax returns

▶ recoup child-support debt from tax returns.

Some may say that prenuptial agreements defeat the purpose of marrying based on the values of love and trust, but they are a good preventive measure against a bad egg. Love hurts but divorce can be expensive. Make sure you consult a lawyer before drafting up any such agreement.

☀ **Tip**

While it is tempting not to lodge income tax returns for a number of years to avoid any increase of child support payments, you could be missing out on a number of other benefits (including substantial tax refunds and government concessions) or simply accruing extra late lodgement penalties with the ATO.

 Death

Three things in life are certain — taxes, death ... and taxes on death! Unlike other countries, there is no gift or inheritance tax in Australia. But don't be fooled because certain transactions that occur as a consequence of a person's death are taxed.

Date of death return

Executors of deceased estates are required to finalise the tax affairs of the deceased person, including any outstanding tax returns.

The final personal tax return of the deceased person with their personal TFN is known as the 'date of death return' and covers the period from the previous 1 July to the date of death. It should include all assessable income derived by the deceased person and all the tax-deductible expenses incurred up to the date of death.

The general individual tax rates, with the full tax-free threshold, apply to the final tax return as well as the Medicare levy and Medicare levy surcharge. Any compulsory Higher Education Loan Program (HELP) or Student Financial Supplement Scheme (SFSS) repayments are also included, but the remaining accumulated HELP debt is cancelled.

Tip

Ordinary losses as well as capital losses will lapse at the time of death and cannot be carried forward into the deceased estate. If possible, try to use these capital losses prior to death by selling any assets that have appreciated in value.

Deceased estate returns

Income derived after the date of death, and any deductible expenses incurred after the date of death, are included in the deceased estate's trust return. Tax returns will need to be lodged in future years until the estate is fully administered and no longer deriving income.

Tax fact

A new tax file number is required to lodge a deceased estate's tax return.

For the first three tax returns, deceased estate income — to which no beneficiary is presently entitled — is taxed at the general individual rates, with the benefit of the full tax-free threshold. No Medicare levy is payable. In the fourth and subsequent years, the concessional period is not extended and special progressive trust tax rates will then apply, as set out in table 1.4.

Table 1.4: deceased estate tax rates (2015–16)

Deceased estate taxable income (no present entitlement)	Tax rates
$0–$416	Nil
$417–$670	50% of the excess over $416
$671– $37 000	$127.30 + 19% of the excess over $594
$37 001–$80 000	$7030 + 32.5% of the excess over $37 000
$80 001–$180 000	$21 005 + 37% of the excess over $80 000
$180 001 and over	$58 005 + 45% of the excess over $180 000

Source: © Australian Taxation Office for the Commonwealth of Australia.

Beneficiaries

A beneficiary is a person who receives all or part of the deceased estate. There may be some tax obligations for beneficiaries, depending on the nature of any distribution they may receive. If the trust distribution consists of:

▶ *Corpus.* There is no tax payable.

▶ *Income.* Tax is payable at the beneficiary's marginal tax rate.

▶ *Assets.* There may be capital gains tax on subsequent disposal; see p. 134 and p. 160.

 Pitfall

Funeral expenses are not tax-deductible, nor are they eligible for the medical expenses tax offset.

13 *Trusts*

Trusts are an excellent vehicle for managing and preserving your family's wealth. They provide a great deal of flexibility in sharing the tax burden as income and capital can be distributed among beneficiaries in the most tax-effective manner. Beneficiaries generally have no legal entitlement or interest in the trust's assets until the date stated in the trust deed (for example, Billy is only entitled to the assets upon reaching age 30).

> ### ☼ Tip
>
> If you are worried about certain family members 'blowing' all of the assets that you worked hard accumulating over the years, the creation of a trust will give you a bit more peace of mind.

Trusts are ideal for those beneficiaries who are hopeless with money, suffer from drug addiction, have long-term health problems or are likely to experience a relationship breakdown in the future. Essentially, family assets can be protected from 'creditors and predators'.

The two main types of trusts used by families are:

▶ *Discretionary trusts.* These are often set up either to hold property and investments on behalf of family members or to operate a business.

▶ *Testamentary trusts.* These are created via a clause in the 'testament' (or will) of an individual, but don't get established until after the individual dies.

A testamentary trust is an indirect way of managing your family's wealth after your death. While you obviously won't be around to oversee the management of the trust itself, you will have some comfort knowing that your loved ones will be looked after financially and not savaged by the ATO.

Tax fact

There are substantial tax advantages relating to testamentary trusts, including distributions to minors being taxed at the more favourable adult rates.

Pitfall

The cost of establishing and maintaining a trust can be high and may outweigh any benefits in having a trust structure, especially when the assets involved are not worth much.

The trustee is the legal owner of the trust property, and is responsible for managing the trust fund on behalf of the beneficiaries. The trustee has a legal duty to obey the terms of the trust deed and to always act in the best interests of the beneficiaries. A trust can operate for up to 80 years in Australia, though it is common to have a clause within the trust deed to allow the trustee the option of winding it up earlier if considered appropriate. Distributions must be documented by 30 June each year.

Pitfall

The ATO takes a dim view of trustees who have distributed net income 'on paper' to certain tax-advantaged beneficiaries (such as companies) but have not physically received any payments from the trust.

Tax fact

There are many benefits to using trusts to manage your wealth, including:

▶ *Asset protection*. Family assets may be protected from 'creditors and predators' in the event of bankruptcy or insolvency in certain situations.

▶ *Australia-wide*. A trust established under Australian law can operate effectively in every Australian state. If you have potential beneficiaries living overseas, it is recommended that you seek specialist advice before proceeding further as there are many tax implications to consider.

▶ *Flexibility*. Trust deeds are flexible in their operation and can cater for a wide variety of beneficiary classes and investments, and different types of income can be directed to different beneficiaries.

▶ *Little regulation*. Trusts do not have as many reporting requirements and obligations as company structures.

▶ *Tax minimisation*. Income can be directed to family members on lower tax rates.

Tip

If you place money in a term deposit, consider having it mature after 30 June so that any income is not assessable until the following financial year.

Part II

Your employment

There have been a few noticeable changes in employment conditions in recent years. Employees seem to be working longer hours as employers seek greater productivity. Employees also seem to be bearing the greater brunt of expenses as employers have become more cost-driven and hence a lot less generous in reimbursing work-related expenses.

> **!**
>
> **Tax fact**
>
> Of the 12.78 million people who lodged a tax return in 2012–13, more than 8.5 million claimed $19.76 billion in deductions for work-related expenses.

Fortunately, employees can claim for work-related expenses in their income tax return each year and get a refund at their marginal rate of tax.

Tax fact

If you work in one of the following occupations or industries, make sure you look at the relevant ATO publication on claiming specific work-related expenses in your tax return:

- ▶ adult industry workers
- ▶ airline employees
- ▶ Australian Defence Force members
- ▶ building and construction workers and earthmoving plant operators
- ▶ cleaners
- ▶ education professionals
- ▶ electricians
- ▶ engineers
- ▶ factory workers
- ▶ fitness and sport industry employees/professional footballers
- ▶ hairdressers
- ▶ hospitality industry employees
- ▶ IT/business professionals
- ▶ journalists
- ▶ lawyers
- ▶ mechanics
- ▶ mining site employees
- ▶ nurses, midwives and direct carers
- ▶ performing artists
- ▶ police informants
- ▶ police officers
- ▶ real-estate industry employees
- ▶ sales representatives and sales and marketing managers
- ▶ security guards
- ▶ shop assistants
- ▶ travel agents
- ▶ truck drivers.

Part II will look at tax deductions that you might be able to claim in relation to your employment income, who the ATO targets, and ways to improve your cash flow and tax situation.

14 *Car usage*

Taxpayers who use their car in the course of earning assessable income may be entitled to claim deductions for some of the costs.

The ATO has outlined that you can claim the cost of using your car to travel:

▶ from your normal workplace to an alternative workplace — for example, a client's premises — while still on duty, and back to your normal workplace or directly home

▶ from your home to an alternative workplace for work purposes and then to your normal workplace or directly home.

 Tip

To help justify your claim for car travel, have client travel included as one of your requirements in your job description or contract of employment.

You *cannot* claim the cost of normal trips between home and work as the expense is private. You cannot claim it even if:

▶ you do minor tasks — such as picking up the mail on the way to work

▶ you have to travel between home and work more than once a day

▶ you are 'on call' and your employer contacts you at home to come in to work

▶ there is no public transport near where you work

▶ you work outside normal business hours — for example, shift work or overtime

▶ your home is a place of business and you travel directly to a place of employment.

You can claim the cost of trips between home and work where:

▶ you use your car because you have to carry bulky tools or equipment that you use for work and there is no secure place for you to leave them at work

▶ your home is a base of employment — you start your work at home and travel to a workplace to continue the work

▶ you are an itinerant worker with shifting places of employment.

Example

Danielle works for a department store in the city and is required to attend a meeting at her employer's other store in the suburbs and travels in her own car. As the meeting finishes late she travels directly home from the meeting. She can claim the cost of the journey from the city store to the suburban store and from the alternative workplace to her home.

The following three characteristics will assist you in determining if your work is itinerant:

▶ travel is a fundamental part of your work

▶ you have a web of workplaces in your regular employment with no fixed place of work

▶ you regularly work at more than one site each day before returning home.

Example

David is employed as a plumber's labourer and works at different sites each day. He travels directly from home to a different site each day to start work. The travel between sites on a regular basis is an integral part of his job and thus his employment would be considered by the ATO to be itinerant.

However, a builder's labourer who works at a single building site for a few months before moving on to another site is not engaged in itinerant work.

 Pitfall

Common mistakes made with car claims include:

▶ a lack of evidence to support claims
▶ providing a 'rough estimate' of your business usage
▶ deductions being incorrectly claimed for the costs of travel between home and work.

FAQ

I am a painter by trade and recently purchased a brand new ute. I work full time and carry my gear with me at all times. I want to know what I can claim, and if I have to keep a log book even though I use my vehicle 100 per cent for work.

Given that you have a ute (commercial vehicle greater than 1 tonne) and clearly carry paint gear all the time, there is no requirement to maintain a logbook as it would be considered 100 per cent work use. However, if you want to use the logbook method then you will need to keep all receipts throughout the year for expenses such as petrol, registration, insurance, servicing and repairs as well as any finance payments (lease or interest).

15 Methods to claim car travel

There are four specific methods available to individuals to calculate deductions for car expenses:

▶ cents per kilometre method

▶ logbook (12-week) method

▶ 12 per cent of original value method

▶ one-third of actual expenses method.

The first two methods are most commonly used, while the last two are used in less than 2 per cent of cases and are proposed to be discontinued for the 2015–16 tax year and beyond.

Tip

If you often use your car for work, the logbook method is probably your best option for calculating deductions.

If you use the logbook method, purchase a logbook from the newsagent, fill it out for a continuous 12-week period and keep records of all costs associated with the running of your car including petrol, registration, insurances, servicing, repairs, lease payments, batteries, tyres, and so on. The hard work is worth it as deductions can be in the thousands and you only need to do a new logbook every five years unless you change your job or car.

Under the logbook method, you can claim a portion of the running costs of the car, including depreciation and interest, based upon your work-related use percentage.

Pitfall

The ATO does check logbooks for their authenticity and a common error is a lack of evidence to support a claim. Each work-related business trip must be entered at the end of the journey (or as soon as possible afterwards) and show:

▶ the date
▶ kilometres travelled
▶ opening and closing odometer readings
▶ the purpose of the journey.

Under the cents per kilometre method, you must make a reasonable estimate of kilometres travelled, up to a maximum of 5000, and multiply this by the rate prescribed by the ATO depending on the size of your car. Table 2.1 shows these rates. It was proposed in the 2015 federal budget that a flat rate of 66 cents per kilometre will apply from the 2015–16 income year, regardless of engine capacity.

Table 2.1: cents per kilometre rates based on engine capacity (2014–15)

Engine capacity — car	Engine capacity — rotary	Cents per kilometre
1600 cc (1.6 litre) or less	800 cc or less	65 cents
1601–2600 cc	801–1300 cc	76 cents
Over 2600 cc	Over 1300 cc	77 cents

Source: © Australian Taxation Office for the Commonwealth of Australia.

You need to satisfy the tax office that the travel was undertaken for income-producing purposes and that your claim is calculated on a reasonable basis. Do not guess!

Example

George is a mechanic who is required to travel regularly to pick up spare parts from a supplier. In his tax return, he guesses that he travelled 3500 kilometres.

A check with George's employer reveals that the trip to the supplier is an 8 kilometre round-trip journey, made no more than three days per week and that George also had four weeks' holidays during the year.

George has not made a reasonable estimate and the claim should have been based on 1152 kilometres (three days × 8 km × 48 weeks). Based on a two-litre engine, the deduction that can be claimed is $876 (1152 km × 76 cents).

! Tax fact

Under the logbook and one-third of actual expenses methods, you can claim fuel and oil costs on either your actual receipts or an estimate based on odometer readings from the start and the end of the year.

16 *Travel*

If you incur travel expenses in the course of your work, or in travelling between one place of business and another, they are deductible, for example motor vehicle expenses, air, bus, train or taxi fares and car rental costs. Accommodation and meals on business trips away from home may also be deductible.

Pitfall

Passport fees and travel insurance are generally considered to be private in nature and are not deductible.

 Tip

If you want to claim travel expenses, you need to keep a travel diary. This applies to work-related trips interstate or overseas of more than five days. It must detail dates, places, times and duration of activities and travel. It's also a good idea to keep business cards of contacts you meet and, even better, give a presentation or a report on your trip when you get back to work that includes this information.

There are special substantiation requirements to making a successful travel tax claim.

A travel diary is a separate record of activities undertaken during travel. Its purpose is to show which of the activities were for income-producing purposes so that an appropriate classification can be made between deductible and non-deductible expenses. An activity is recorded by specifying its:

▶ date and approximate start time

▶ duration

▶ location

▶ nature.

Note that the requirement to keep travel records in the form of a diary is separate from the requirement to obtain written evidence of travel expenses.

Tax fact

Sometimes taxpayers mix business with pleasure and it is not uncommon to tack on a personal holiday at the end of an overseas conference. However, travel expenses related to attending conferences, seminars and other work-related events are deductible only to the extent that they relate to your income-producing activities.

You will need to apportion your travel expenses where you undertake both work-related and private activities. Travel costs to and from an overseas conference will only be deductible where the main purpose of the travel was to attend the event. Accommodation, food and other incidental costs must be apportioned between work-related and private activities taking into account your activities on the day you incurred the cost.

Pitfall

Travel expenses for your spouse and family accompanying you while on work-related travel are non-deductible. If any expenses are not separately identifiable, then they will need to be reasonably apportioned between private and deductible.

Some employers pay a travel allowance to cover expenses for accommodation, food, drink or incidentals incurred by an employee while travelling away from home overnight. If your employer does this and the allowance is less than the reasonable travel allowance published by the ATO, you can claim a deduction for the amount of the allowance without further substantiation.

> 💣 **Pitfall**
>
> If you claim an amount greater than the 'reasonable travel allowance amount', the whole claim, not just the excess, must be substantiated.

17 *Uniform*

The cost of certain types of work clothing may be deductible, as can the cost of buying or replacing clothing, uniforms and footwear. But a deduction is only available if the clothing is one of the following:

▶ protective

▶ a compulsory uniform to be worn for work

▶ a non-compulsory uniform that has been entered on the Register of Approved Occupational Clothing.

Tax deductions for the costs of washing, drying or ironing clothes are only available for clothing that falls into one or more of the above categories.

If you do your own laundry you can claim $1 per load if the load is made up only of eligible clothes. This reduces to 50 cents per load if other laundry items are included. If your total laundry costs exceed $150 you must be able to substantiate your claim.

All other expenditure on clothing and its maintenance is considered a private expenditure and is not deductible.

Tip

A deduction for uniformed clothing is only available if it is protective clothing or compulsory, unique and distinctive. Non-compulsory uniforms must be entered on the Register of Approved Occupational Clothing in order to be deductible.

There must be a clear connection between the clothing expenditure and income-earning activities in order to obtain a deduction. In general you cannot claim a deduction for conventional clothing that forms part of a uniform even if your employer requires you to wear it.

Example

A businessman wearing a business suit and tie or a sales assistant working for a big fashion label and wearing one of their tops as a condition of employment are not wearing clothes that are deductible.

Clothing purchased by a taxpayer is considered conventional if it is not distinctive or unique, can be worn on any occasion, including private and social occasions, and is easily available to the public.

Pitfall

Work uniform expenses are a deduction where taxpayers often make mistakes, including:

▶ not keeping receipts for dry cleaning and uniform purchases to support their claim

▶ trying to claim for clothing expenses that are conventional and not unique, distinctive or compulsory

▶ not having a sufficient nexus between their clothing and how it relates to earning income.

Bonus resources

Go to my website www.mrtaxman.com.au for a work-related uniform expenses calculator.

18 *Home office*

More and more people these days are doing work at home as an easy remedy to balance the conflicting pressures of work and family. If you perform some of your work from your home office, you may be able to claim a deduction for the costs you incur in running your home office, even if the room is not set aside solely for work-related purposes.

You may be able to claim the work-related portion of:

▶ depreciation of home-office furniture, fittings and equipment such as computers and desks — if your equipment costs less than $300, you can claim a full deduction for the work-related portion

▶ home telephone calls

▶ home telephone rental if

 ☐ you are on call

 ☐ you have to phone your employer, clients or students regularly while you are away from your workplace

▶ internet access charges

▶ printer and printer cartridges

▶ stationery

▶ the cost of heating, cooling and lighting your home office that is over the amount you would ordinarily have to pay if you did not work from home

▶ the costs of repairs to your home-office furniture and fittings.

 Tip

Sit at your desk at home and scan the room for the various items that you may use, even partially, for work purposes.

Example

Shelby uses her computer and personal internet account at home to access her work emails and to grade student assignments in the following percentages:

▶ 35 per cent for work purposes

▶ 65 per cent for private purposes.

This means Shelby can claim 35 per cent of both the depreciation of her computer and her internet costs.

 Pitfall

If your income is paid to you as an employee, you are generally not able to claim a deduction for your occupancy expenses including:

▶ council rates

▶ home insurance premiums

> ▶ mortgage interest
> ▶ rent.
>
> You can only claim occupancy expenses where your home office is considered to be a place of business.

According to the ATO, to claim a deduction for electricity and gas and the decline in value of home-office furniture you can use either of the following:

▶ your actual expenses

▶ a rate of 34 cents per hour.

 Tip

Keep a diary (for a minimum of four weeks) to record the amount of time you use your home office for work purposes. You can then apply the 34 cents per hour method for determining a deduction for electricity, gas and depreciation of home-office furniture.

Example

Michelle uses a diary to record the time she uses her home office for work purposes. Based on her diary entries, Michelle works out that she spends an average of four hours each weeknight working in her home office. Michelle works for 46 weeks each year.

Michelle calculates her home office running expense deduction as follows:

46 weeks × 20 hours × 0.34 cents = $312.80

Bonus resources

Go to my website www.mrtaxman.com.au for a home office expenses calculator to help you work out how much you can claim.

19 Other work-related deductions

Other work-related expenses that you incur as an employee that haven't been mentioned previously may include:

▶ briefcases

▶ calculators and personal organisers

▶ diaries and logbooks

▶ first-aid courses

▶ income-protection insurances

▶ interest on money borrowed to finance work-related purchases

▶ mobile phones

▶ overtime meal expenses

▶ postage

▶ professional seminars, courses, conferences and workshops

▶ reference books

▶ stationery

► subscriptions

► sun protection

► technical journals, periodicals and magazines

► tools of trade

► union fees.

 Tip

The records you must keep to substantiate your claims include:

► receipts or other written evidence of your expenses, including receipts for depreciating assets you have purchased

► diary entries you make to record your small expenses ($10 or less) totalling no more than $200, or expenses that you cannot obtain any kind of evidence for, regardless of the amount — for example, stationery

► itemised phone accounts that detail work-related calls — if you don't receive itemised accounts, you can make a reasonable estimate of your call costs based on diary records you have kept over a four-week period, together with your relevant telephone accounts.

Example

Lucy uses her mobile phone for work purposes. She is on a mobile phone plan of $49 per month and rarely exceeds the plan cap. She reviews an itemised account for one month from her phone provider, which includes details of the individual calls she has made. She highlights the work-related calls she has made and makes notes on her account about who she is calling for work and personal purposes — her employer, parents and so on.

(continued)

Example *(cont'd)*

She works out that 45 per cent of the individual call expenses are for work and applies that to her cap amount of $49 a month. Reviews of other months are consistent with this.

If Lucy only worked for 26 weeks of the year, she would calculate her work-related mobile phone expense deduction as follows:

$$6 \text{ months} \times \$49 \times 0.45 = \$132$$

 Tip

It is better to get your employer to pay for as many work-related expenses as possible rather than claiming them yourself. Based on the marginal tax rates, you only get back a percentage of any expense incurred, not 100 per cent of the expense. Avoid leaving yourself out of pocket.

 Pitfall

If you have purchased any assets that cost more than $300 you must depreciate them rather than claim the full amount as an immediate deduction.

 FAQ

Can you claim for expenses incurred that have been purchased via the National Disability Insurance Scheme?

Unfortunately you cannot claim deductions for expenses incurred (or for assets purchased) in relation to any exempt income, including amounts received from the NDIS.

20 *Keeping those receipts*

It is crucial that you keep your receipts, particularly as the ATO increases its audit activity all the time. With the ATO motto of 'no receipt means no deduction' you could be missing out on legitimate tax deductions by not keeping good records.

Under the Australian tax system of self-assessment you are responsible for working out how much you can claim on your tax return. In order to prepare an accurate tax return and support the claims you make, you need to keep careful records.

Personally I don't care what system you use to keep your receipts…just have one. The system that works will be organised into various categories to allow you to find a receipt within five minutes if asked.

Most accountants prefer that you don't give them a shoebox each year, but instead a typed-up summary, perhaps in Excel, of your income and expenses. Their tax agent fees may even fall as a result!

If you're not sure whether or not to keep a record, you should keep it — it is better to have too many than not enough.

 Tip

It doesn't matter what system you use to keep your tax receipts, just make sure you use one! An Excel spreadsheet showing your income and expenses works for many people.

If your total claims add up to more than $300, you must keep written evidence, such as receipts, bank statements and credit card statements. You must be able to show evidence you have incurred the full amount of your claim, not just the amount over the first $300.

Written evidence should show:

▶ amount of the expense

▶ date you incurred the expense

▶ nature of the goods or services—if this is not shown, you can write this on the document before you lodge your income tax return

▶ supplier's name.

If the total amount you are claiming is $300 or less, you do not need to keep receipts.

 Pitfall

Even if you hold onto the original receipt, there is no tax deduction available if you have been reimbursed by your employer.

Generally, you must keep your written evidence for five years from:

▶ the date the notice of assessment is sent to you

▶ the date of your last claim for any decline in value for depreciating assets

▶ disposal of an asset for CGT purposes

▶ the date a dispute with the ATO is finalised.

Tax fact

Taxpayers with 'simple tax affairs' only need to retain their records for two years if:

▶ their income consists only of salary or wages, interest or dividends within Australia

▶ deductions are only for managing tax affairs, bank fees or donations.

Documents that you are required to keep can be in written or electronic form. If you make copies they must be a true and clear reproduction of the original.

 Pitfall

If you keep records electronically, be very careful about not losing that data. A regular back-up is essential to ensure that the evidence is easily accessible if a hard drive is corrupted or a computer stolen.

---

21 *ATO hit lists*

Every year, based on an analysis of previous returns, the ATO issues a 'hit list' of occupations that will be targeted for close attention regarding work-related expenses.

Tax fact

The ATO's tactic of putting the spotlight on particular groups has proven successful in past years. When the ATO targets particular industries, its tax collection improves by 22 per cent.

Generally the ATO looks closely at a range of claims for deductions including expenses for motor vehicles, self-education and travel. It also looks at tax returns from previous years and identifies particular occupations to put under the microscope where:

▶ average amounts of claims are high

▶ there is an increase in the number of people making claims

▶ there are a lot of people making claims for the first time.

In the spirit of 'prevention is much better than cure', the ATO uses that information and writes to people in those occupations. It sends information outlining common mistakes made in claims, and provides help on how people can get their claims right in the subsequent year's tax return.

 Pitfall

The ATO is aware that email addresses they have been using since July 2012 have been sending out scam emails. The emails appear to be from an @ato.gov.au email address and display as being sent from the 'Australian Tax Office'. If you have received emails from this source do not open the attachment and delete the email immediately. If the ATO needs to contact you they will only do so via the phone or post.

 Tip

While the natural tendency of people in targeted occupations is to reduce the amount of their claims out of fear, if you are genuinely entitled to a legitimate tax deduction then you should claim it. By all means go to the boundary, but not over it. If you are concerned about your claims then you should seek advice from a tax expert.

The first step in a subsequent ATO investigation usually involves a 'please explain' letter requesting further information about your tax return.

Usually a person is given 28 days to respond and the ATO might also ask for copies of receipts and other supporting documents. Only if the matter remains unresolved after this is a face-to-face meeting required.

You will be given lots of opportunity to explain yourself. But the penalties are significant so it's best to have all your affairs in order. Penalties start from a minor adjustment to your return if there was a genuine mistake or misinterpretation of the law, and escalate to severe fines.

💣 Pitfall

If you make a downright fraudulent claim for, say, $20 000 and there is no substance at all to it, the ATO can charge up to 90 per cent tax in penalties, plus an interest penalty on top of that.

Tax fact

The ATO has outlined some simple rules for getting your work-related expenses claim correct:

▶   You must have incurred the expense in the year you are claiming for.

▶   The expense must be work-related and not private.

▶   Receiving an allowance from your employer does not automatically entitle you to a deduction.

▶   If your claims total more than $300 you need written evidence.

Penalties that the ATO can charge as a percentage of any tax shortfall are 75 per cent for intentional disregard of a tax law; 50 per cent for recklessness; and 25 per cent when you don't take reasonable care, if your case is not reasonably argued or if you disregard a private ruling by the ATO. These penalties are increased by a further 20 per cent of the base amount if you do not cooperate and make it difficult for the ATO when looking at your affairs (for example, the penalty for intentional disregard of a tax law when you don't cooperate becomes 90 per cent, being 120 per cent of the base penalty of 75 per cent). The Commissioner encourages voluntary disclosure so if you confess your sins during an audit investigation they will reduce the base penalty amount by 20 per cent. If you advise of any errors prior to any audit activity, then the base penalty amount is reduced by 80 per cent.

> **Tax fact**
>
> In 2012–13, the ATO spent $106.1 million on legal costs relating to litigation against taxpayers.

22 Redundancy

Over the past five years there has been plenty of uncertainty in the global economy with many people still experiencing job losses as the fallout from the global financial crisis (GFC) continues.

If there can be any good news it relates to your favourable tax treatment if you have been dismissed from your employment and received a genuine redundancy payment.

> **Tax fact**
>
> The ATO has outlined that a genuine redundancy payment is one received by an employee, under age 65, who is dismissed from employment because the employee's position is genuinely redundant and:
>
> ▶ the payment being tested is received because of an employee's termination
> ▶ that termination involves the employee being dismissed from employment
> ▶ that dismissal is caused by the redundancy of the position
> ▶ the redundancy payment is made genuinely because of a redundancy.

Tax-free component of genuine redundancy

Part of a genuine redundancy is tax-free and must be taken in cash. The tax-free limit for the 2015–16 income year is $9780 plus a further $4891 for each completed year of service.

Balance of redundancy

Anything in excess of the tax-free amount is treated as an 'employment termination payment'. The first $185000 (increasing to $195000 in 2015–16) is taxed at 17 per cent if you are over 55, or 32 per cent if you are under 55. Any excess payment is taxed at 47 per cent. These tax breaks will only apply to the part of a payment that, when combined with other taxable income, does not exceed $180000.

 Tip

The balance of a genuine redundancy can be rolled over into your superannuation fund as a personal contribution and is then concessionally taxed at only 15 per cent within the fund.

Unused leave entitlements

Only 5 per cent of any unused annual or long-service leave that relates to service prior to 16 August 1978 is taxed at your marginal rate. If you leave employment because of a genuine redundancy, invalidity or early retirement scheme, then the balance is taxed at 32 per cent. You cannot roll any unused leave entitlements over into your super fund. Note that the tax calculation on unused leave entitlements is different if you leave employment for any other reason.

Example

Natalie, aged 51, is made redundant on 30 June 2015 after working at her company since 15 February 2005. Her company pays her $130 000 as a genuine redundancy plus her unused leave entitlements, which come to another $31 234.

As she has given the company 10 full years of service, the tax-free component of her genuine redundancy is $58 960 ($9780 + [$4891 × 10]) and the balance of $71 310 is an employment termination payment.

As she is only 51, and doesn't elect to roll over any money into her super fund, the $71 310 is taxed at 32 per cent; that is, $22 819. Her unused leave entitlements are taxed at 31.5 per cent; that is, $9995.

 Pitfall

While most payroll departments get redundancy and termination calculations correct, occasionally they get them wrong. And when they get them wrong ... they can get them horribly wrong. I have seen calculations that have been out by $38 000! It pays to have a tax expert look at the calculations.

23 *Working a second job*

Tax problems always seem to occur when you start working a second job. If you are an Australian resident for tax purposes, the first $18 200 of your yearly income is not taxed. This is called the tax-free threshold. You can claim the tax-free threshold from one payer only when you complete your TFN declaration (NAT 3092).

You should claim the tax-free threshold with the payer who pays the highest wage. If you earn any additional income from a second job your other payer is required to withhold tax at a higher rate.

If you are currently claiming the tax-free threshold with a payer and you want to claim it from a new payer, you must advise your first payer that you no longer wish to claim the tax-free threshold by completing a withholding declaration (NAT 3093).

Pitfall

If you claim the tax-free threshold from your second payer it may lead to a tax debt at the end of the financial year. Money can be very hard to find once you have spent it.

Where an insufficient amount of tax is being withheld, you can directly instruct a payer to withhold a higher amount of tax, by supplying them with a completed *Withholding declaration — upwards variation* (NAT 5367) form. However, if your payer is withholding tax at the prescribed rates, you are under no obligation to increase the amount of tax being withheld. You suffer no penalty at the end of the financial year, other than having to find a further amount of money to pay your tax.

Example

Stuart is employed in two part-time jobs. He receives $30 000 from the first job and $18 000 from the second job. Using the ATO's *Pay-as-you-go (PAYG) withholding — Fortnightly tax table* (NAT 1006), the tax withheld on Stuart's wages is outlined in table 2.2 (overleaf).

(continued)

Example *(cont'd)*

Table 2.2: example—tax withheld

	Annual income	Fortnightly income	Tax withheld
First job	$30 000	$1 153.85	$134
Second job	$18 000	$692.31	$130
Total	$48 000	$1 846.16	$264

Source: © Australian Taxation Office for the Commonwealth of Australia.

At the end of the financial year Stuart's net tax position is:

Income tax on $48 000	$7147
Medicare levy (2%)	$960
Total tax payable	**$8107**
Less: tax withheld ($264 × 26)	$6864
Net tax shortfall	**$1243**

To avoid this situation, Stuart can either put money aside for when his income tax assessment is issued or choose to ask one or both of his employers to withhold extra tax to cover the shortfall.

If you think you are having too much tax withheld from one of your wages, you can arrange for a PAYG withholding variation form to be completed and reduce the amount withheld from your regular pay. Or wait until the end of the year and get a nice refund.

 Tip

When you have a second job you may be able to claim the cost of travelling directly between two separate places of employment. However, you can't claim the cost of travelling from your second job to your home.

24 *Salary sacrifice*

It is quite common for employees to set up a salary-sacrifice arrangement with their employer and 'package' some of their future salary or wages in return for benefits of a similar value provided by their employer. These benefits may include superannuation and fringe benefits such as company cars, private health insurance and other expense payments.

Tax fact

Your income tax liability should be less under a salary-sacrifice arrangement than it would have been without entering into the agreement. It is important to note, though, that there are some associated costs that you need to consider before entering into any arrangement. These costs may include the opportunity cost of the amount being sacrificed plus any surcharges which may arise after having the benefits reported on your payment summary.

Provided that any benefits form part of your remuneration, there is no limit on the amount or the types of benefits that can be sacrificed. They are simply replacing what otherwise could have been paid as salary.

 Tip

Superannuation, exempt fringe benefits and some car fringe benefits are generally the best forms of salary sacrifice for tax purposes.

Salary-sacrificed superannuation contributions under an effective salary-sacrifice arrangement are considered to be employer contributions and are taxed at 15 per cent (increasing to 30 per cent for individuals with income greater than $300 000), subject to contribution limits, within the fund. This is a lot more tax-effective than paying 49 per cent tax on your cash salary, if you are on the highest marginal tax rate.

 Tip

If you are a high-wealth individual who runs your own business via a company structure, consider staying under the $300 000 threshold by keeping funds inside the corporate entity rather than drawing a wage or a dividend. If you do need to draw out beyond the threshold, consider taking a 'hit' in one financial year but stay under for the ones around it.

Make sure that you agree to all the terms of any salary-sacrifice arrangement with your employer, preferably in writing and before starting any work. A contract of employment is a good place to detail the arrangement. You can renegotiate a salary-sacrifice arrangement at any time, such as in renewable contracts.

The ATO is known to frown upon any arrangements put into place after the work has been performed, and arrangements that are not in writing. You are allowed to have a verbal agreement but you may have difficulty establishing the facts of your arrangement should the tax man conduct an audit of your affairs.

Salary sacrifice implications for employees include:

▶ Income tax is paid on the reduced salary or wages.

▶ Your employer may be liable to pay fringe benefits tax (FBT) on the non-cash benefits he or she provides and is likely to adjust your remuneration accordingly.

▶ Salary-sacrificed superannuation contributions are classified as employer superannuation contributions (rather than employee contributions) and are taxed at 15 per cent in the superannuation fund (increasing to 30 per cent for individuals with income greater than $300 000).

▶ There should be no access to the sacrificed salary; it must be permanently forgone for the period of the arrangement.

▶ Your employer may be required to report certain benefits on your payment summary that also need to be disclosed in your annual income tax return.

> ### 💣 Pitfall
>
> Your earnings base, on which your compulsory superannuation contributions are calculated, may be reduced if you salary sacrifice your super, unless your arrangement states otherwise.

25 *Fringe benefits*

A fringe benefit is a benefit either you or an associate, such as your spouse or children, receive because of your employment. If there is any fringe benefit tax (FBT) payable on the benefits received, your employer is liable to pay that tax. You only pay income tax on your reduced salary. But as part of your salary-sacrifice agreement your salary may be reduced by the amount of FBT paid by your employer.

Common fringe benefits include:

▶ car parking

▶ cars

▶ expense payments

- ▶ housing
- ▶ loans
- ▶ meals and entertainment
- ▶ property.

Tax fact

Employees of certain not-for-profit organisations receive generous FBT concessions. The FBT cap on exempt benefits provided by public and not-for-profit hospitals and public ambulances is $17 667. This cap will increase to $31 177 for public benevolent institutions (except hospitals) and health promotion charities.

Tax fact

The following—limited to one per year—are exempt benefits:

- ▶ briefcase
- ▶ computer software
- ▶ portable electronic device (unlimited for small businesses from 2016–17)
- ▶ protective clothing
- ▶ tools of the trade.

There are two alternative methods to calculate the FBT for cars:

- ▶ Logbook—based on actual usage over a 12-week period completed in the past five years.

- ▶ Statutory method—based on the total number of kilometres travelled and applying a statutory fraction to the cost of the car provided. Table 2.3 shows the fractions that apply and have been replaced with a flat rate of 20 per cent for all cars acquired after 1 April 2014.

Table 2.3: car fringe benefits statutory formula rates (2015–16)

Travel (kms)	Statutory fraction of car base value Date contract entered into				
	Before 11/5/11	11/5/11 – 31/3/12	1/4/12 – 31/3/13	1/4/13 – 31/3/14	After 1/4/14
0–14 999	26%	20%	20%	20%	20%
15 000–24 999	20%	20%	20%	20%	20%
25 000–40 000	11%	14%	17%	20%	20%
40 001 and over	7%	10%	13%	17%	20%

Source: © Australian Taxation Office for the Commonwealth of Australia.

! Tax fact

Ways to reduce FBT may include the following:

▶ Make an employee contribution towards the cost of the benefit.

▶ Keep a logbook.

▶ For cars acquired before 10 May 2011, travel more and get into a lower statutory fraction bracket.

▶ Consider getting a commercial vehicle (exempt).

▶ Return the car and keys to your employer when you are not using the car for extended periods, such as holidays.

Reportable fringe benefits amounts are certain fringe benefits greater than $2000 which are included in your payment summary and shown in your tax return, but not included in your assessable income. They are included in a number of income tests for certain government benefits including:

▶ Medicare levy surcharge

▶ deductions for personal super contributions

▶ super co-contributions

▶ spouse super contributions

▶ mature age worker tax offset

▶ HELP and Financial Supplement repayments

▶ child-support obligations.

Example

Table 2.4 illustrates the way salary sacrificing and employee contributions work. Aaron earns $74 000 a year. He has a car purchased for $40 000 which has annual running expenses of $15 000. If he travels 22 000 kilometres during the FBT year, the taxable value of the car fringe benefit will be $8000 (20 per cent × $40 000) and he will need to sacrifice one of the following:

▶ $22 094 without any employee contributions
▶ $7000 if employee contributions of $8000 are made.

Table 2.4: example — salary sacrifice

	1 Salary only (no packaging)	2 Salary + car (without employee contributions)	3 Salary + car (with employee contributions)
Annual remuneration	$74 000	$74 000	$74 000
Less salary sacrifice	Nil	$22 094	$7000
Taxable income	**$74 000**	**$51 906**	**$67 000**
Less income tax	$15 597	$8416	$13 322
Less Medicare levy	$1480	$1038	$1340
Income after tax/ salary sacrifice	**$56 923**	**$42 452**	**$52 338**

	1 Salary only (no packaging)	2 Salary + car (without employee contributions)	3 Salary + car (with employee contributions)
Less employee contribution	Nil	Nil	$8000
Less car expenses	$15 000	Nil	Nil
Net disposable income	**$41 923**	**$42 452**	**$44 358**
Reportable fringe benefits amount (taxable value × 1.8868)	Nil	$15 094	Nil

Source: © Australian Taxation Office for the Commonwealth of Australia.

! Tax fact

According to the ATO, it takes the average business 11.3 hours to complete its annual fringe benefits tax return.

26 Living-away-from-home allowance

The ATO defines a living-away-from-home allowance (LAFHA) as a taxable allowance that an employer pays to an employee to compensate for additional expenses incurred and any disadvantages suffered because the employee is required to live away from their usual place of residence in order to perform their employment-related duties.

You are considered to be living away from your usual place of residence when:

▶ you change your job location (but not your employer)

▶ you intend to return to your original location after time away

▶ the period away exceeds 21 days.

As a practical general rule, where the period away does not exceed 21 days, the allowance will be treated as a travelling allowance rather than as a LAFHA.

FBT is only payable on the amount that the LAFHA exceeds the exempt accommodation and food components.

Tax fact

Since 1 October 2012, access to the tax concessions for the LAFHA is limited to a 12-month period for an employee at a particular work location.

Since 1 October 2012, LAFHA can only be claimed by people who maintain a home for their own use in Australia that they are living away from for work. In addition, the LAFHA concession can only be used for the expenses of people who are legitimately maintaining a second home in addition to their actual home for a maximum period of 12 months. For those Australian residents who had an employment arrangement in place before 8 May 2012 (that has not been materially varied), then the new LAFHA rules have been applicable since 1 July 2014.

You have not made a material change to your employment arrangement if:

▶ your salary is adjusted as a result of an annual salary review (or other annual adjustments are made)

▶ you are promoted and the underlying terms of your employment arrangement do not change.

Accommodation

The exempt accommodation component of the LAFHA is the amount you pay for additional accommodation expenses you could *reasonably* be expected to incur at the alternative location. The ATO doesn't have any strict guidelines concerning what is considered 'reasonable accommodation', but it mainly boils down to common sense. Factors you could take into account when determining the accommodation cost include:

▶ whether you will be accompanied by family members

▶ the position you hold

▶ the location where you will be living

▶ whether the accommodation will be furnished

▶ your current living standards.

 Pitfall

If an employee does not spend all of the LAFHA provided for accommodation, the excess is not an exempt accommodation component and is taxable for FBT purposes.

Food

The exempt food component is the amount of the LAFHA that is compensation for expenses you could *reasonably* be expected to incur on food and drink because you must live away from your usual place of residence, less the statutory food amount of $42 a week for each adult and $21 a week for each child.

> **Tax fact**
>
> There are no strict guidelines as to how the food component is calculated, provided the amount is reasonable. You could determine reasonable food costs using the rates the ATO publishes each year for expatriates, providing they are reasonable in your circumstances. The acceptable amounts for the reasonable food component in the 2015–16 financial year of LAFHAs for expatriate employees, per ATO Tax Determination 2015/7, are as follows:
>
> ▶ one adult $241
> ▶ two adults $362
> ▶ three adults $483
> ▶ one adult + one child $302
> ▶ two adults + one child $423
> ▶ two adults + two children $484
> ▶ two adults + three children $545
> ▶ three adults + one child $544
> ▶ three adults + two children $605
> ▶ four adults $604
> ▶ additional adult $121
> ▶ additional child $61.

Pitfall

From 1 October 2012, 457 visa holders do not satisfy the requirement of maintaining a home for their own use in Australia while they are living away from it. As a result, they are not able to claim deductions for accommodation and food, but will still need to include any allowance received as assessable income. For those 457 visa holders who had an employment arrangement in place before 8 May 2012 (which has not been materially varied), then the new LAFHA rules have been applicable since 1 July 2014.

Tax fact

If you are an employee who works on a 'fly-in fly-out' or a 'drive-in drive-out' basis (such as a miner), then you are not subject to the same 'maximum 12 months' LAFHA rule. You will still need to substantiate your accommodation and food expenses if they are more than the ATO's reasonable amounts.

Part III

Your education

Contrary to what many property experts and stockbrokers may tell you, the best investment that you could make is in yourself. With the economy recovering there are going to be some great opportunities in the job market for those who have acquired more skills. You are never too old to learn new tricks and, as my old man would say, nobody can take your education away from you.

> **Tax fact**
>
> Of the 570 000 taxpayers that claimed for self-education expenses in 2012–13, 79 per cent earned less than $80 000 for the year.

Australia is in the midst of an education revolution and pushing for more highly skilled workers. Tax and government incentives are helping fill the classrooms of universities and technical and further education (TAFE) colleges around the country with part-time students every evening. Employers are also expecting more from their employees and encouraging them to study in conjunction with their work.

> ### ☼ Tip
>
> If you are planning to claim self-education expenses, be sure that the course you are claiming specifically relates to a current income-producing role, not one you hope to have in the future.

This part focuses on the financial implications and government incentives around studying.

> ### Bonus resources
>
> Go to my website www.mrtaxman.com.au for a self-education expenses calculator to give you an estimate of the deduction you can claim for work-related self-education expenses.

27 Claiming self-education expenses

Work-related self-education expenses are the costs you incur to undertake a work-related course of study at a school, college, university or other recognised place of education.

> **Tax fact**
>
> The ATO says a tax deduction for your self-education expenses is available if you work and study at the same time, the course has sufficient connection to your current employment, and it *either*:
>
> ▶ maintains or improves the specific skills or knowledge you require in your current employment
> *or*
> ▶ results in, or is likely to result in, an increase in your income from your current employment.

According to the ATO, if a course of study is too general in terms of your current income-earning activities, the necessary connection between the self-education expense and your income-earning activity does not exist.

> **Pitfall**
>
> The ATO is quite strict in its view on self-education expense deductions. A deduction for self-education expenses cannot be claimed for a course that does not have a sufficient connection to your current employment even if the course:
>
> ▶ is generally related to your current employment
> ▶ enables you to get new employment.

Provided there is sufficient connection between your course and employment at the time you incurred the expense, the following self-education expenses are allowable tax deductions:

▶ accommodation and meals, only when participating in your course requires you to be away from home for one or more nights

▶ computer expenses, including interest to finance them

▶ depreciation of the cost of your computer, professional libraries, desks, chairs, filing cabinets, bookshelves, calculators, technical instruments, tools and other equipment (such as desk lamps)

▶ photocopying

▶ running expenses if you have a room set aside for work-related study purposes — such as the cost of heating, cooling and lighting that room while you are studying in it

▶ self-education expenses paid with your Overseas Study — Higher Education Loan Program (OS-HELP) loan

▶ stationery

▶ student union fees

▶ textbooks, professional and trade journals

▶ travel expenses between your home (or work) to your place of education and back

▶ tuition fees, including fees payable under FEE-HELP.

 Tip

If you have a room set aside for work-related study purposes, you can claim a fixed rate of 34 cents per hour of usage instead of keeping individual costs for heating, cooling, lighting, cleaning and decline in value of furniture.

You cannot claim a tax deduction for:

▶ accommodation and meals associated with day-to-day living expenses

▶ repayments you make (whether compulsory or voluntary) on debts you may have under the following loan schemes:

　□　HECS-HELP

　□　FEE-HELP

　□　OS-HELP

　□　Student Financial Supplement Scheme (SFSS)

▶ self-education expenses such as tuition fees paid under HECS-HELP

▶ last stage of your travel between home, work and place of education.

Bonus resources

Go to my website www.mrtaxman.com.au for a self-education expenses calculator to give you an estimate of the deduction you can claim for work-related self-education expenses on your tax return.

28　The $250 threshold

Based on the formula for calculating your claim for work-related self-education expenses, in certain circumstances you may have to reduce your allowable self-education expenses by $250. The different categories of expenses are outlined in table 3.1 and the formula is as follows:

Total self-education expenses claim
= A − [$250 − (C + D + E expenses)] + B + C + D

Table 3.1: categories of self-education expenses

Category	Allowable expenses
A	tuition fees, textbooks, stationery, student union fees, public transport fares, car expenses worked out using the 'logbook' or 'one-third of actual expenses' method, running expenses for a room set aside specifically for study
B	depreciation deductions such as a computer, desk or car for which you are claiming a deduction in Category A
C	repair costs to assets used for work-related study
D	car expenses using the 'cents per kilometre' or '12 per cent of original value' method; you cannot claim car expenses under this category if you have included deductions for decline in value or repairs to your car under categories B or C
E	expenses you have incurred but cannot use as a deduction

Source: © Australian Taxation Office for the Commonwealth of Australia.

Example

Matthew has an accounting cadetship with a firm in the city and attends university in the evenings. His textbooks for the year cost $320 and he also catches a bus from work to university, which costs him $80 per annum. As his costs incurred were $400, Matthew can only claim $150 after the $250 reduction.

Tax fact

If the total of (C + D + E expenses) is greater than $250 it is reduced to 0, not a negative amount.

If you have other expenses that are not allowable as a deduction (see category E), you can offset them against the $250 before you have to reduce the amount you can claim.

Tax fact

Under Australian tax law the first $250 of self-education expenses is not deductible. But certain self-education expenses you have incurred — but are not allowed as a deduction — can be used to offset the $250 reduction including:

▶ capital costs of items acquired in the financial year and used for work-related study purposes, such as a computer or desk
▶ child care costs related to attendance at lectures or other work-related study activities
▶ travel expenses for the last stage of travel from *either*:
  ☐ your home to your place of education and then to your workplace
    or
  ☐ your workplace to your place of education and then to your home.

29 *Self-development courses*

Over the past few decades we have seen a rise in the number of self-development courses that cover a range of different topics, most of which are not tax-deductible. Just like with university and TAFE courses, the ATO will only allow you to claim a deduction for expenses relating to courses that have a sufficient nexus with your income-producing activities.

There has also been a dramatic increase in the number of 'success seminars' where thousands sit in an audience for one or two days and listen to a presenter on the big stage. They are short, intense programs without the active involvement that would be expected from a TAFE or uni student. As a result, the ATO considers the material covered by these seminars as being too generic and not specific enough to a taxpayer's income-earning activities.

Some topics are clearly private in nature, such as diet and nutrition, intimate relations and meditation.

Likewise, self-development courses can have a strong philosophical or spiritual component, can be undertaken over months or years and can often be offered by correspondence.

 Pitfall

Fees for courses on personal development or life-coaching programs are not generally deductible as the link between your current employment and the program is not clear enough—the course is considered to be essentially personal in nature.

Other topics are too general in scope to be classed as income-related, such as communication skills, decision making and getting along with others.

 Pitfall

If a course is too general or the skills you learn over-qualify you for your current position, there is not enough of a connection between your self-education expense and your employment.

The ATO outlines that to be eligible for a deduction for expenses you incur for a self-improvement or personal development course, the course must have a sufficient connection to your current employment and *either*:

▶ maintain or improve the specific skills/knowledge you require in your current employment
  or
▶ result in, or be likely to result in, an increase in your income from your current employment.

Tax fact

A tax deduction can be claimed when you undertake a self-improvement or personal development course that includes modules or elements that can be directly related to your current income-earning activities. Allowable topics that are sufficiently specific to be classed as income-related include:

▶ leadership
▶ leading change
▶ mentoring staff
▶ project management.

Personal or executive coaching may be considered income-related if the series of regular discussions between the participant and a coach have a strong income-related focus. If the program has a strong focus on finding the participants' goals and directions, and on their work-life balance, then income-related material is barely covered.

The amount of the deduction you can claim will be determined by the extent to which the course is directly related to your current income-earning activities.

Example

Suzie is a manager who undertakes a self-development course consisting of the following five modules, all of equal value and cost:

- ▶ communication
- ▶ getting on with others
- ▶ handling change
- ▶ leadership
- ▶ mediation.

The module on leadership would be classed as income-related, but the remainder of the modules are private or too general in nature to be tax-deductible. As the income-related content makes up 20 per cent of the course, Suzie can only claim a deduction for 20 per cent of the costs that she incurs in undertaking the course.

30 *Higher Education Loan Program*

University students are generally a pretty poor bunch who struggle to pay for next week's rent let alone afford to pay their course fees. So the Higher Education Loan Program (HELP) was introduced to provide a loan to assist students to pay for their university tuition.

While there is no interest rate as such, a consumer price index (CPI) adjustment is effectively charged on HELP debts on 1 June each year. According to the ATO, the average HELP debt among 1.823 million taxpayers is $15898.

Once you start working and your income is above a minimum repayment threshold, you must make compulsory repayments, which the ATO works out via your income tax assessment, as outlined in table 3.2.

Table 3.2: HELP repayment thresholds and rates (2015–16)

HELP repayment income (HRI*)	Repayment rate
Below $54 126	Nil
$54 126–$60 293	4%
$60 294–$66 457	4.5%
$66 458–$69 950	5%
$69 951–$75 191	5.5%
$75 192–$81 433	6%
$81 434–$85 719	6.5%
$85 720–$94 332	7%
$94 333–$100 520	7.5%
$100 521 and above	8%

*HRI = taxable income plus any total net investment loss (which includes net rental losses), total reportable fringe benefits amounts, reportable super contributions and exempt foreign employment income.

Source: © Australian Taxation Office for the Commonwealth of Australia.

 Proposed change

It was announced in the 2014–15 federal budget that the government will reduce the income threshold for repayment of HELP debts commencing in 2016–17 by 10 per cent (with a repayment rate of 2 per cent) and will also adjust the indexation of HELP debts from 1 June 2016 to a rate equivalent of the yield on 10-year government bonds (up to a 6 per cent maximum) instead of the current CPI.

Tip

If you only work full time during university holidays or part time while studying, then ask your employer not to withhold additional amounts for HELP or SFSS debts (see p. 86), provided that you do not expect to earn above the annual repayment thresholds. If your employer continues to deduct these amounts, then you should lodge your income tax return as soon as possible in order to get your tax refund.

 Tax fact

HELP debts are not extinguished if you go overseas or become bankrupt. Even on death, the executor of your estate must lodge all outstanding tax returns and the estate is liable for any compulsory repayments that relate to the period before your death. Only then is the remainder of the accumulated debt cancelled by the ATO.

If you make a voluntary repayment of $500 or more you will receive a bonus of 5 per cent credited to your account.

Proposed change

Proposed changes in the 2013–14 federal budget removing the 5 per cent bonus on any voluntary repayment have not been passed at date of publication.

Example

Hamish has accumulated a HELP debt of $23 567. He makes a voluntary repayment of $20 000 towards his debt. He receives a $1000 discount, being 5 per cent of the repayment, reducing his HELP debt to $2567.

Tip

If lodging your tax return would result in clearing your HELP debt in full, then consider, provided you have the available funds, making a voluntary repayment to get the 5 per cent discount.

 Bonus resources

Go to my website www.mrtaxman.com.au for a HELP voluntary repayment calculator to give you an estimate of the bonus you will receive when you make a voluntary repayment towards your HELP debt and the amount that will remain after you've made your voluntary repayment.

💣 **Pitfall**

Making a voluntary repayment reduces your debt immediately. However, you may still have to make a compulsory repayment if:

▶ you still have an accumulated HELP debt
▶ your repayment income is above the minimum compulsory repayment threshold.

FAQ

I have a HELP debt and am working two jobs while I study but I expect to earn only $25 000 from those jobs (well under the threshold for needing to make a HELP repayment) although for my second job, they are withholding approximately $150 each fortnight

(continued)

from my pay. Will I get all this back when I lodge my tax return and will the ATO see that I have earned under the threshold?

As your income will be under the repayment threshold, the ATO will not calculate any HELP debt repayments when they assess you at the end of the year. That may not necessarily mean that you will get a nice refund at the end of the year because the $150 tax being deducted each fortnight is going into a general pool of tax deducted. If enough tax is not being taken out of the second job (due to double claiming the tax-free threshold as an example) then the ATO will use the excess HELP deductions to cover this shortfall.

31 Student Financial Supplement Scheme

The Student Financial Supplement Scheme (SFSS) was a voluntary loan scheme to help tertiary students cover their expenses while studying. While the scheme was closed in 2003, the ATO continues to collect existing financial supplement debts through the tax system.

As with HELP debts, a CPI adjustment is effectively charged on SFSS debts on 1 June each year. Once your income is above a minimum repayment threshold, you must make compulsory repayments that the ATO works out via your income tax assessment, as outlined in table 3.3.

Table 3.3: SFSS repayment thresholds and rates (2015–16)

Repayment income (RI*) thresholds	Repayment rate
Below $54 126	Nil
$54 126–$66 457	2%
$66 458–$94 332	3%
$94 333 and above	4%

*RI = Taxable income plus any total net investment loss (which includes net rental losses), total reportable fringe benefits amounts, reportable super contributions and exempt foreign employment income.

Source: © Australian Taxation Office for the Commonwealth of Australia.

Bonus resources

Go to my website www.mrtaxman.com.au for an SFSS repayment calculator to help you work out your compulsory SFSS repayment.

However, unlike for HELP debts, there is no bonus if you make a voluntary repayment against your SFSS debt.

FAQ

I have an SFSS debt. If I die, does my debt get passed to my next of kin or is it voided completely?

Your estate will need to lodge a final 'date of death' tax return and repayments for SFSS will be calculated normally as in any other tax year. However, you can die peacefully knowing that any remaining SFSS (or HELP) debt will be written off by the government and you will not be leaving any huge debts to your family.

Tax fact

You may be able to defer your compulsory HELP or SFSS repayment, for up to one year, if you can show that *either*:

▶ making your repayment has caused, or would cause you, serious hardship
   or
▶ deferring your repayment is fair and reasonable for other special reasons.

Bonus resources

You can apply to defer your HELP or SFSS compulsory repayment by completing the *Deferring your compulsory HELP, HECS or Financial Supplement repayment* application form (NAT 2471), available on the ATO website.

32 *Austudy and* ABSTUDY

Austudy

Austudy is a government benefit paid by Centrelink that provides financial help for students and apprentices. If you are either studying an approved full-time course at an approved institution or undertaking a full-time Australian apprenticeship and are aged 25 or over, then you may be eligible for Austudy. Approved courses for Austudy purposes include full-time secondary education courses, graduate courses, undergraduate courses and some masters, diplomas and TAFE courses. If you have already completed a masters degree or a doctorate, then this is likely to disqualify you from any payment, regardless of satisfying the above criteria. Both income and assets tests need to be satisfied in order to receive Austudy. Unlike the Youth Allowance, there is no parental means test requirement.

Income test

You can earn up to $427 per fortnight (before tax) and receive the full Austudy entitlement. The payment is reduced by 50 cents in the dollar if your income is between $427 and $512 and by 60 cents in the dollar when you earn above $512 per fortnight. If you are receiving Austudy, you must report your employment income to Centrelink every fortnight, even if you are not paid in some fortnights.

Assets test

As an applicant for Austudy you will be assessed against an assets test, depending on age and home-ownership.

As at May 2015, single homeowners must have assets other than their home worth less than $202 000 in order to satisfy the assets test for Austudy entitlements (and most other government allowances and pensions), rising to $348 000 for single non-homeowners. For couples, the combined assets limit is $286 500 for those that own a home, rising to $433 000 for those that do not. These couples limits also apply where illness may separate spouses.

 Proposed change

It was announced in the 2015–16 federal budget that the assets test threshold for a single homeowner will increase to $250 000 from 1 January 2017 and $375 000 for a homeowner couple. These thresholds will increase by $200 000 for non-homeowners ($450 000 for single and $575 000 for couple non-homeowners).

Tip

Visit the Department of Human Services website www.humanservices .gov.au for the most up-to-date information on the asset test limits for allowances and full pension entitlements. Figures are updated four times each year, in January, March, July and September.

Austudy is not payable if your assets exceed these amounts. Even if you satisfy the assets test, payments may still be deferred if your liquid assets (such as cash, shares and term deposits) exceed $5500 if you are single, or $11 000 if you are a couple or single with dependants.

Tax fact

There are other government payments and benefits that you may be entitled to if you receive Austudy, including:

▶ advance payment
▶ fares allowance
▶ low-income health care card
▶ pharmaceutical allowance
▶ remote area allowance
▶ rent assistance
▶ student start-up scholarship.

ABSTUDY

ABSTUDY is a government allowance that is similar to Austudy and is available to Indigenous secondary or tertiary students or full-time Australian apprentices, as an incentive to stay at school or in further study. Those students and apprentices of

Australian Aboriginal or Torres Strait Islander descent or who identify as an Aboriginal or Torres Strait Islander person (and are accepted as such by their community) may be eligible for ABSTUDY.

💣 Pitfall

A tax deduction for self-education expenses is not available if the only income you received was from one of the following:

► Austudy
► ABSTUDY
► similar payments providing financial assistance.

Tax fact

The ATO will not allow any deduction for self-education expenses against any government assistance payments, including Austudy and ABSTUDY.

Bonus resources

If you wish to check your eligibility for Austudy or ABSTUDY, go to www.centrelink.gov.au for more information.

---

33 Trade Support Loans

The Trade Support Loans (TSL) program was introduced in 2014 to encourage more young people to commence a trade and complete their qualification.

Eligible Australian apprentices can receive a lifetime loan limit of $20 000 (indexed with inflation from 1 July 2017) over four years to assist with everyday costs while they complete their apprenticeship over a four-year period.

To be eligible for Trade Support Loans payments, apprentices must:

▶ reside in Australia and be an Australian citizen, or the holder of a permanent visa;

▶ be undertaking a:

    ☐ Certificate III or IV level qualification that leads to an occupation on the National Skills Needs List; or

    ☐ Certificate II, III or IV agricultural qualification; or

    ☐ Certificate II, III or IV horticulture qualification while working in rural or regional Australia; and

▶ meet the eligibility criteria that is assessed by the Australian Apprenticeships Centre on receipt of a Trade Support Loans Application Form.

There are no age restrictions for applying for a Trade Support Loan.

Tax fact

Under the TSL, eligible Australian apprentices can access up to $8000 in their first year, $6000 in the second, $4000 in the third and $2000 in the fourth year. If apprentices have not reached their $20 000 lifetime limit after four years, they may also receive up to $2000 per annum in subsequent years.

Tip

Upon successful completion of an apprenticeship, Australian apprentices will be entitled to a 20 per cent discount on the loan.

Similar to HELP loans for tertiary students, the loans become repayable once apprentices start earning a particular amount of income.

The TSL debt is repaid through the tax system once your repayment income is above the minimum repayment threshold for compulsory repayment.

The repayment rates and thresholds are the same as those for the Higher Education Loan Program (HELP). For the 2015–16 income year, the minimum repayment threshold is $54 326.

Tax fact

The Trade Support Loans program is administered by the Australian Apprenticeships Centre and the Department of Industry. For more information go to www.australianapprenticeships.gov.au

34 *Scholarships*

How scholarships are structured will determine if they are taxable or tax-free.

Scholarships are exempt from income tax when a full-time student at a school, college or university receives a stipend for a scholarship, bursary, educational allowance or other educational assistance.

However, the principal purpose of the scholarship must be the education of the student.

Tax fact

Scholarship payments are exempt from income tax if:

▶ they are made to a full-time student at a school, college, TAFE or university

▶ they are made by way of scholarship, bursary, educational allowance or educational assistance

▶ it is accepted that selection to receive a scholarship is merit-based and that the scholarship has the requisite educational purpose.

● Pitfall

Beware of promoters who offer to help you to set up a scholarship fund to pay for your children's education with the promise that the arrangement will minimise your tax. The ATO has announced that these arrangements are not genuine scholarships as students are not independently selected on a wide range of criteria and that any scholarship payments under these arrangements are taxable in the hands of the student.

Some scholarships, bursaries, grants and awards are taxable, including education benefits provided under a friendly society scholarship plan.

Tax fact

Scholarship payments are subject to income tax if they are payments made:

▶ by the Commonwealth for education or training
▶ to part-time students
▶ under a scholarship that does not have merit-based selection
▶ on condition that the student will (or will if required) become an employee of the payer
▶ on condition that the student will (or will if required) enter into a contract with the payer that is wholly or principally for the labour of the student
▶ under a scholarship that is not provided principally for educational purposes.

If you are not sure about the tax consequences of a scholarship payment, contact the organisation that paid you.

Tax fact

If your scholarship is taxable you should advise your payer that your scholarship is assessable income—they will need to withhold tax (PAYG) from your periodic payments. You will need to show your scholarship amount as assessable income in your tax return.

 Pitfall

If you have a family trust and distribute some of the net income to your child's school to cover their school fees then do so at your peril. The ATO views these transactions as a way to try and avoid tax and will generally assess tax on the trustees of the family trust at 47 per cent of the amount paid to the school.

35 *School building funds*

Many parents make payments to school building funds but they are not necessarily tax-deductible.

For a gift to a school building fund to qualify for a tax deduction, it must have the following characteristics:

▶ made voluntarily

▶ amounts to $2 or more

▶ made to a school building fund that is endorsed as a deductible gift recipient (DGR)

▶ made to a school building fund that is maintained solely for providing money for acquiring, constructing or maintaining the school or college buildings

▶ put towards a building, or group of buildings, used for a purpose that is connected with the curriculum of a school or college by a non-profit organisation

▶ does not provide a material benefit to the donor (such as a reduction in school fees, tickets to functions or the grant of scholarships to nominated students)

▶ essentially arises from benefaction.

 Pitfall

Compulsory payments to a school building fund are not deductible. They are essentially a levy and part of the total school fees.

The ATO will not allow deductions for building funds that are for sports grounds, tennis courts, covered play areas, car parks, landscaping, furniture or equipment. However, the ATO would allow deductions relating to the building of an indoor sports complex on school grounds (where it includes a gym, basketball court and an in-ground swimming pool) as it is a permanent structure forming an enclosure providing protection from the elements.

A multipurpose building is taken to be used as a school or college if the primary and principal use of the building (more than 50 per cent of the time) is as a school or college.

Example

A hall used by a school every weekday by students and teachers and for community meetings at weekends would qualify as a school or college building. If the hall was used as a basketball court for external groups only it would not be considered a school or college building.

Donors need to keep records of their deductible gifts for tax record-keeping purposes. Receipts for gifts must state the name of the fund, authority or institution to which the gift has been made, the DGR's Australian business number (if any) and the fact that the receipt is for a gift.

Example

Alain voluntarily gives $700 cash to a school building fund that is a DGR. He can claim an income tax deduction for $700 because:

▶ it is made to a DGR
▶ the payment is a gift
▶ a payment of money falls within one of the gift types
▶ there are no gift conditions for school building funds.

Pitfall

A deduction for a gift to a school building fund cannot add to or create a tax loss for a taxpayer.

Tax fact

Over 4.55 million individuals claimed just over $2.29 billion in donations in the 2012–13 financial year. As at October 2014, there were 60460 tax concession charities and 28100 deductible gift recipients in Australia.

Bonus resources

For more information for people wanting to claim a tax deduction for gifts to school building funds (or for organisations wanting to establish them), the ATO has recently released Taxation Ruling *TR 2013/2 Income tax: school or college building funds.*

36 *Education savings plans*

Having a savings plan for your kids' education is a brilliant idea and something that every responsible parent should start as early as possible. As you probably already know, the cost of raising and educating a family isn't cheap.

Tax fact

According to the Australian Scholarship Group, parents of children born in 2015 can expect to spend between $71 406 (government) to $541 275 (independent) on education by the time the class of 2032 graduates from Year 12.

 Tip

Friendly societies usually issue education savings plans. They are great in terms of creating discipline (by encouraging regular deposits and restricting withdrawals) and they can be tax-effective. However, check their investment returns prior to investing because sometimes they can be poor.

In order to be tax-free, education savings plans need to be issued for the sole purpose of providing 'education benefits' for nominated students and not used as security for borrowing or raising money.

Any withdrawals of funds that relate to contributions made are considered capital in nature and therefore tax-free. However, the student must include in his or her assessable income any withdrawals of funds that relate to investment income on those contributions. With the higher tax-free threshold and the low-income tax offset, it would be expected that there would be no tax to pay on any payments made to students in the year that they turn 18 (and subsequent years) as they are assessed under adult tax rates.

Pitfall

If education benefits are paid before the nominated student turns 18, then any investment income may be assessed at their unfavourable minor tax rates.

Benefits that are withdrawn and used for an expense that is not directly related to the nominated student's education will be treated as 'non-education benefits'. In that event, the ATO deems the recipient to be the member and not the nominated student. This benefit will be treated similarly to the proceeds of a 10-year bond for which the following rules apply:

▶ No personal tax is payable on withdrawals after 10 years subject to a 125 per cent further contributions tax rule (where the total amount of contributions paid during a year increases by no more than 125 per cent of the total contributions in the previous year).

▶ If a withdrawal is in the first eight years, the growth component is assessable but a 30 per cent tax offset applies to offset the personal tax impact.

▶ If the withdrawal is within the ninth year, only two-thirds of the growth is assessable, with only one-third assessable if withdrawn in the tenth year. The 30 per cent tax rebate is also available on withdrawals in those years, and is calculated on the assessable portion.

 Tip

Once your child has left school and no longer has a need for the education savings plan, consider keeping and contributing to the bond as you will continue to reap the tax benefits associated with the bond reaching its 10-year anniversary.

37 *Other government assistance*

Aside from HELP, Austudy, ABSTUDY and the Youth Allowance, there are other government benefits that provide financial assistance while you are studying.

HECS-HELP benefit

The HECS-HELP (Higher Education Contribution Scheme — Higher Education Loan Program) benefit was introduced on 1 July 2009 to encourage maths, science, education or nursing (including midwifery) graduates to take up employment in specified occupations. Further, it encourages early-childhood education graduates to work in specified locations including rural and regional areas, Indigenous communities and areas of socioeconomic disadvantage.

Tax fact

The HECS-HELP benefit is not a cash payment, but a reduction to your compulsory HELP repayment or, if you do not have to make a compulsory repayment, a reduction to your accumulated HELP debt. For the 2014–15 income year, the benefit is up to $1878.93 for early childhood education teachers, and $1761.49 for maths, science, education and nursing (including midwifery) graduates. On 1 June each year, indexation is applied to these maximum benefit amounts to maintain their real value in line with the cost of living, as measured by the consumer price index (CPI).

You may apply for the benefit each income year you are employed in an eligible occupation for a total lifetime claim of 260 weeks for each type of benefit. Claims do not have to be in consecutive years.

 Pitfall

You have two years from the end of the income year for which you are applying to submit your HECS-HELP benefit application. For example, applications for the 2014–15 income year must reach the ATO by 30 June 2017.

FEE-HELP

FEE-HELP is a loan for eligible fee-paying students enrolled at an eligible higher education provider or Open Universities of Australia.

The government has defined a limit to help pay for all or part of your tuition fees. The FEE-HELP limit, indexed each year, is the total amount available to you under both FEE-HELP and Vocational Education and Training FEE-HELP (VET FEE-HELP). In 2015, the FEE-HELP loan limit is $97 728, except for medicine, dentistry and veterinary science courses where the limit is $122 162.

VET FEE-HELP

Vocational Education and Training (VET) FEE-HELP is a student loan scheme for the vocational education and training sector and is part of HELP. VET FEE-HELP assists eligible students undertaking certain VET diploma, advanced diploma, graduate diploma and graduate certificate courses of study at an approved VET provider.

Tip

If you take out a FEE-HELP or VET FEE-HELP loan to pay your tuition fees, you may be entitled to a tax deduction for the cost of your tuition fees.

OS-HELP

Overseas Study HELP (OS-HELP) is a loan that helps students meet airfares, accommodation costs and other travel expenses while undertaking some of their study overseas.

Tip

If you take out an OS-HELP loan to pay costs associated with overseas study, you may be entitled to claim a tax deduction for some of the costs.

Pitfall

You cannot claim a tax deduction for repaying all or part of your FEE-HELP, VET FEE-HELP or OS-HELP loan. These loans become part of your accumulated HELP debt and are collected through the tax system once your repayment income is above the minimum repayment threshold. Voluntary and compulsory repayments are not tax-deductible.

Youth Allowance

The Youth Allowance is a government benefit paid to eligible students, apprentices or those looking for work aged 16 to 24. It is means tested based on both the young person's income and his or her parents' income. The allowance is assessable and must be included in your income tax return. Unfortunately, Youth Allowance recipients cannot claim a tax deduction for expenses incurred in relation to their studies.

Part IV

Your investment property

Almost one in every four taxpayers in Australia owns a rental property. Aside from increasing their financial wealth, many people invest in property to enjoy the tax benefits.

> **!**
>
> **Tax fact**
>
> Over 1.94 million people claimed more than $41.98 billion in rental deductions in their tax returns in the 2012–13 tax year.

While rental income is assessable, outgoings relating to your investment property are allowable deductions and can be offset against other income. This will generally result in a tax refund for the taxpayer. So the more that you can claim as allowable deductions, the lower your taxable income becomes and the higher your refund.

Tip

If you own a rental property with someone else, you need to show your share of the rental income and expenses in your income tax return in the same proportion as shown on the legal title of the property.

For those who proceed down the investment property track, a big part of the available tax deduction is the interest portion of the mortgage. Other costs that can be claimed include property management fees, rates, loan costs and maintenance and repairs.

In part IV we will focus on how to maximise the tax benefits of owning a rental property as well as looking at ways to minimise any CGT liability in the future.

 Pitfall

Rental properties have been on the ATO's watch list for a few years now because the sizes of the tax deductions are significant and they are a haven for errors. Each year, the ATO makes contact with many thousands of taxpayers with rental properties and asks them to explain and justify what they put in their tax return. Make sure that you can justify your claim.

Common mistakes include not having a depreciation schedule from a quantity surveyor, adding back personal usage of property and claiming capital items as repairs.

38 *Negative gearing*

When expenses relating to an investment property (such as rates, insurance, repairs and interest) are greater than the rent you receive then you are negatively gearing it. The net loss is a deduction in your tax return — against other income such as salary, interest and business income — and will generally result in a refund.

Tax fact

The average net rental loss by Australian taxpayers in the 2012–13 tax year was $9558, while the average net gain for those properties positively geared was $9409.

Example

Table 4.1 is an example of how to calculate your net rental income or loss.

Table 4.1: net rental income or loss

	Scenario 1	Scenario 2	Scenario 3	Scenario 4	Scenario 5
(a) Assessable income before rent	$200 000	$200 000	$100 000	$70 000	$35 000
Rental income	$9300	$9300	$9300	$9300	$9300
Rental expense	$20 600	$20 600	$20 600	$20 600	$20 600
(b) Net rental loss	$11 300	$11 300	$11 300	$11 300	$11 300
(c) Taxable income (a − b)	$188 700	$188 700	$88 700	$58 700	$23 700
(d) Marginal tax rate	49%	47%	39%	34.5%	21%
(e) Tax benefit of negative gearing (b × d)	$5537	$5311	$4407	$3899	$2373
(f) Net cash outflow by investor (b − e)	$5763	$5989	$6893	$7401	$8927

Due to the progressive tax system in Australia, negative gearing is more beneficial to people in the higher income brackets who pay tax at the top marginal rate. But over the years, as tax brackets have changed and tax rates reduced, there are actually fewer people in the top tax bracket who can take full advantage of negative gearing benefits. In the above example, the taxpayer in the highest tax bracket (scenario 1) gets a tax refund of $5537. But if they were in the 21 per cent tax bracket (scenario 5), then they would only get $2373 back and be out of pocket by $8927. The worst scenario is where the other income is not sufficient to absorb the rental property loss. In this instance there is no tax refund, but the loss can be carried forward to following tax years.

Tip

Don't let emotion take over when you are buying a house because there is too much at stake financially if you get too attached and go over your budget. You may end up with a property that is too highly negatively geared and struggle to meet the minimum repayments.

I am not a big fan of negative gearing as most people become asset rich but cash poor under this strategy. People who invest in several properties actually struggle to pay for them out of their cash flow. Negative gearing means that your expenses exceed your revenue so automatically your cash flow is negative. The tax benefit is still only a percentage of that loss.

Pitfall

Negative gearing strategy is not the be all and end all. When making an investment decision, make sure that you follow the 'ABC motto' — 'Absolute Bloody Cash!'

While the example (on p. 108) shows different taxpayers getting nice refunds (ranging from $2373 to $5537), they are still out of pocket by the net cash outflow figure. The capital value of their properties must increase by at least that amount each year, otherwise they are falling further behind financially than they were at the start of the year.

The only situation in which you would negatively gear a property is when the capital growth of your property is greater than the negative cash outlay. Of course there are no guarantees that this is going to happen.

☼ Tip

A positively geared rental property, where the rent received is greater than your property expenses, provides a better financial result after tax than a negatively geared property. Of course you need to pay tax, but I would happily pay $5537 in tax if I knew that my bank account increased by $11300 without any effort!

 Interest

If you take out a loan to purchase a rental property, you can claim the interest charged on that loan, or a portion of the interest, as a deduction. It is generally the biggest tax deduction for rental property investors.

Tax fact

According to ATO statistics, interest claims represented more than 53.7 per cent of the total claims made by taxpayers for rental property deductions in the 2012–13 tax year.

While your property is rented, or available for rent, you may also claim interest charged on the loan you used to:

▶ finance renovations (such as adding a deck or second floor)

▶ purchase depreciating assets (such as an air-conditioner or stove)

▶ pay for repairs (such as roof repairs due to storm damage).

Tip

All debt is bad debt. But if you are going to have debt, make sure it is tax-deductible debt. Pay off your non-deductible debt (such as personal loans, home loan and credit card) first rather than making extra repayments against loans for investment properties. Once you have paid off all non-deductible debt start looking at extinguishing the tax-deductible debt.

You can also claim interest on loans to purchase land on which to build a rental property. However, if your intention changes—for example, you decide to use the property for private purposes and you no longer use it to produce rent or other income—you cannot claim the interest.

You also cannot claim interest if you:

▶ start using the rental property for private purposes

▶ use a portion of the loan for private purposes (such as purchasing a new car or investing in a super fund)

▶ borrow against an existing rental property to buy a new home to live in.

Example

Joe and Mary decide to take out a $290 000 loan at 6.25 per cent. $260 000 is to be used to buy a rental property and $30 000 to buy a car.

Interest for year 1 = $290 000 × 6.25% = $18 125

Apportionment of interest payment related to rental property:

(continued)

Example *(cont'd)*

Total interest expense × (rental property loan ÷ total borrowings) = deductible interest

$$\$18\,125 \times (\$260\,000 \div \$290\,000) = \$16\,250$$

Joe and Mary can each make an interest claim of $8125 on their respective tax returns for the first year of the property.

Source: © Australian Taxation Office for the Commonwealth of Australia.

 Pitfall

A common mistake is to claim a deduction for interest on the private portion of the loan. The interest expense must be apportioned between the 'deductible' and the 'private' portions of the total borrowings. The calculations can be complicated, particularly if you have a loan account that has a fluctuating balance due to a variety of deposits and withdrawals and it is used for both private purposes and rental property purposes.

If you use the equity on your existing property to buy a new house to live in, you cannot claim the interest on the additional borrowing even if you rent out the original house that the loan is secured against. Only the portion of the interest that relates to the original loan for the rental property will be deductible in this instance.

 Tip

If you expect your income to be lower next year (perhaps due to maternity leave or redundancy) you should consider prepaying a year's worth of interest in advance before 30 June this year. This strategy will bring forward deductions against the higher income and thus you'll get the tax benefit back at a higher marginal rate of tax.

Tip

Don't overcommit when buying a property. Why do approximately 40 per cent of first home owners currently suffer mortgage stress? Because they purchased beyond their financial means. Make a budget before you buy. Lending organisations have been just as guilty pre-GFC in giving too much. Just because they are willing to give you $1 million doesn't mean that you have to spend it all. A minimum 20 per cent deposit will create a buffer to cater for job losses, family planning and illness, interest rate rises and unexpected costs as well as avoid mortgage insurance. Never rely on a bonus to make regular repayments. It is better to buy a smaller house and live a comfortable life with regular family holidays than have a huge house and not be able to enjoy it because you work overtime and weekends.

FAQ

Can I claim all the interest on an investment property that I own with my wife as I am earning $200 000 (that is, on the highest marginal tax rate) but she is at home with the kids and doesn't earn any other income?

Nice try but unfortunately not. Any expenses for joint properties needs to be apportioned to each owner based on your respective percentages of ownership. The upside is that when you sell the property and have to pay CGT down the track, your wife (assuming her income levels are still low) won't have to pay as much for her share of any gain.

40 *Depreciation*

Behind interest, depreciation is usually the second-biggest deduction available for rental property investors, yet many don't claim it.

As your rental property gets older, the items within it experience wear and tear and they depreciate in value. The ATO allows property investors to claim a deduction for depreciation on:

▸ plant and equipment

▸ renovations or capital improvements commenced after 27 February 1992

▸ the building itself, if built after 18 July 1985.

The amount of the depreciation claim can vary greatly depending on the age, use, fit-out and type of building. Plant and equipment items are basically items that can be 'easily' removed from the property as opposed to items that are permanently fixed to the structure of the building. These include things like carpets, hot water systems, blinds and light fittings. They are usually written off over five to 10 years.

Due to the high deduction available for building costs, if you have bought an investment property and it was built after 18 July 1985, it is definitely worthwhile organising a depreciation schedule from a quantity surveyor.

The ATO has a comprehensive list of more than 230 residential property items that can be depreciated.

Tip

If your investment property was built after 18 July 1985, it is definitely worth organising a depreciation schedule from a quantity surveyor. It takes about three to four weeks to organise a depreciation schedule and costs around $500–600, but you get the benefits back tenfold with tax savings via increased depreciation claims.

The building write-off allowance (known as the capital works allowance) is a 2.5 per cent deduction available, written off over 40 years, for the structural element of a building including fixed, irremovable assets. It is based on historical building costs excluding the cost of all 'plant' and non-eligible items and includes things such as the bricks and mortar, walls, flooring and wiring.

 Pitfall

When you sell your rental property you will need to reduce your cost base, for CGT purposes, by the amount claimed for the building write-off allowance.

There are two methods that can be applied when depreciating property for tax purposes:

▶ prime cost (or straight line)

▶ diminishing value (or reducing balance).

Under the prime cost method the deduction for each year is calculated as a percentage of the cost as follows:

cost × days owned ÷ 365
× 100% plant's effective life (in years)

Under the diminishing value method the deduction is calculated as a percentage of the balance you have left to deduct:

opening undeducted cost × days owned

÷ 365 × 200%* plant's effective life (in years)

*Note: reduce to 150% if item purchased before 10 May 2006.

The ATO specifies the individual effective life for all plant and equipment items. If you claim using the diminishing value method, you are claiming a greater proportion of the asset's cost in the earlier years. If you claim using the prime cost method, you are claiming a lower but more constant portion of the available deductions over the lifetime of the property.

The intentions of the property investor will determine which method will be most suitable for them. My experience shows that most investors employ the diminishing value method, as depreciation deductions under this method are cumulatively higher over the first five years of ownership.

Depreciation is not limited to new properties. If you haven't previously claimed for depreciation, then you can request an amendment to your returns for the missed claims.

 Tip

Ensure that you organise your depreciation schedule for your investment property from a quantity surveyor. They are one of the few professionals recognised by the ATO to have the appropriate construction costing skills to calculate the cost of items for the purposes of depreciation.

41 *Low-value pooling*

In addition to using the diminishing value method, to maximise rental property deductions in the first five years, investors can 'pool' depreciable assets with written-down values less than $1000 and depreciate them at a more favourable 'pool rate' of 37.5 per cent.

 Tip

Provided they are not part of a set, you generally get an immediate deduction for depreciable assets costing $300 or less.

Once an asset is allocated to a low-value pool, it remains in the pool and it is not necessary to work out its adjustable value or decline in value separately. Only one annual calculation is required.

 Pitfall

New assets acquired for less than $1000 during the year are allocated as 'low-cost assets' to the pool but the decline in value for these assets in the first year is at a rate of 18.75 per cent, or half the pool rate. Halving the rate recognises that assets may be allocated to the pool throughout the income year and eliminates the need to make separate calculations for each asset based on the date it was allocated to the pool. For subsequent years they are depreciated at the normal pool rate of 37.5 per cent.

The following example shows how to work out decline-in-value deductions.

Example

In the 2015–16 tax year, Rebecca allocated some depreciating assets she acquired in that year in relation to her rental property to a low-value pool, as shown in table 4.2.

Table 4.2: example of decline-in-value deduction calculations

	Cost or opening adjustable value	Low-value pool rate	Deduction for decline in value
Low-value assets:			
Various	$2679	37.5%	$1005
Low-cost assets acquired:			
Television (purchased 19/9/2015)	$687		
Microwave (purchased 31/3/2016)	$423		
Total low-cost assets acquired	$1110	18.75%	$208
Total deduction for decline in value for year ended 30 June 2016			$1213

Closing pool value at 30 June 2016

$$= \text{Low-value assets} + \text{low-cost assets}$$

$$= (\$2679 - \$1005) + (\$1110 - \$208)$$

$$= \$2576, \text{ which will be depreciated at 37.5 per cent in 2016–17 year}$$

Source: © Australian Taxation Office for the Commonwealth of Australia.

Bonus resources

For more information about low-value pooling, including how to treat assets used only partly to produce assessable income and how to treat the disposal of assets from a low-value pool, the ATO has the excellent publication *Guide to depreciating assets* (NAT 1996).

 Repairs and maintenance

Expenditure for repairs and maintenance is the tax deduction that confuses investors the most. Repairs generally involve a replacement or renewal of a worn-out or broken part and relate directly to wear and tear or other damage that occurred as a result of your renting out the property, such as:

▶ replacing part of the guttering or windows damaged in a storm

▶ replacing part of a fence damaged by a falling tree branch

▶ replacing broken windows

▶ repairing electrical appliances or machinery.

Maintenance is when work is done to prevent deterioration or fix existing deterioration including:

▶ painting a rental property

▶ oiling, brushing or cleaning something that is otherwise in good working condition

▶ maintaining plumbing.

This will generally be deductible if the property:

▶ continues to be rented on an ongoing basis

▶ remains available for rental but there is a short period when the property is unoccupied, such as when unseasonable weather causes cancellations of bookings or advertising is unsuccessful in attracting tenants.

Tax fact

If you no longer rent the property, the cost of repairs may still be deductible provided:

▶ the need for the repairs is related to the period in which the property was used to produce income

▶ you used the property to produce income during the year in which you incurred the cost of repairs.

You can't claim the total costs of repairs and maintenance in the year you paid for them if they did not relate directly to wear and tear or other damage that occurred due to renting out your property.

💣 Pitfall

A common mistake is to claim initial repairs or capital improvements as immediate deductions. Initial repairs to rectify damage, defects or deterioration that existed at the time of purchasing a property are generally considered capital in nature and not deductible, even if you carried them out to make the property suitable for renting. However, these repairs may be claimed as capital works deductions over 40 years.

Capital improvements (such as landscaping, remodelling a bathroom or adding a deck) are non-deductible. This means you cannot claim the entire replacement cost you incurred in the year you incurred it. However, you may be able to claim the cost over a number of years as a capital works deduction or a deduction for decline in value. The cost of repairs to the property that amount to an improvement, and don't merely restore it back to its original condition, is generally capital and not deductible if it:

▶ provides something new

▶ furthers the income-producing ability or expected life of the property

▶ changes the character of the item you have improved

▶ goes beyond just restoring the efficient functioning of the property.

If you have to replace something identifiable as a separate item of capital equipment (such as a complete fence or building, a stove, kitchen cupboards or a refrigerator), you have not carried out a repair.

 Tip

If you conduct a project that includes both repairs and improvements to your rental property, ask for an itemised invoice to help you claim a deduction for the cost of your repairs upfront separately from the cost of the improvements.

Tax fact

If you receive an insurance payout for the cost of repairs, you must include this amount as income on your tax return.

43 Travel to see your investment property

If you travel to inspect or maintain your property or collect the rent, you may be able to claim the costs of travelling as a deduction. You are allowed a full deduction where the sole purpose of the trip relates to the rental property. However, in other circumstances you may not be able to claim a deduction or you may be entitled to only a partial deduction.

The old wives' tale of claiming two trips per year is hogwash. You can claim as many trips as you like so long as the purpose of the trip is to inspect the property and you don't tack a family holiday onto it.

Example

Michael makes a number of visits to his rental property in order to inspect it and to carry out minor repairs. He travelled 222 kilometres during the course of these visits.

On the basis of a cents per kilometre rate of 77 cents for his 2.8 litre car*, Michael can claim the following deduction:

Distance travelled × rate per km = deductible amount

$$222 \text{ km} \times 77 \text{ cents} = \$170.94$$

* See table 2.1 on p. 39 for the appropriate rates.

There is potentially no deduction if the property inspection was merely incidental to the private purpose for the trip.

> **Example**
>
> On his way to golf each Saturday, Michael drives past the property to 'keep an eye on things'. These motor vehicle expenses are not deductible as they are incidental to the private purpose of the journey.

If you fly to inspect your rental property, stay overnight, and return home on the following day, all of the airfare and accommodation expenses would generally be allowed as a deduction provided the sole purpose of your trip was to inspect your rental property.

A common mistake is to claim a deduction for the cost of travel when the main purpose of the trip is to have a holiday and the inspection of the property is incidental to that.

Where travel related to your rental property is combined with a holiday or other private activities, you may need to apportion the expenses. You may be able to claim local expenses that are directly related to the property inspection and a proportion of accommodation expenses.

> **Example**
>
> Paul and Kylie spent $700 on airfares and $1000 on accommodation when they travelled from their home to a resort town, mainly for the purpose of holidaying, but also to inspect the property they own there. They also spent $70 on taxi fares for the return trip from the hotel to the rental property. They spent one day on matters relating to the rental property and nine days swimming and sightseeing.
>
> No deduction can be claimed for any part of the $700 airfares. They can claim a deduction for the $70 taxi fares. A deduction for 10 per cent of the accommodation expenses (10 per cent of $1000 = $100) would be considered reasonable in the circumstances.

(continued)

Example *(cont'd)*

The total travel expenses they can claim amount to $170 ($70 taxi fares plus $100 accommodation). Accordingly, Paul and Kylie can each claim a tax deduction of only $85.

FAQ

If a property is in both my husband's and my names (that is, joint owners) but he is retired and does not pay any tax, can I claim the expense for him to fly to inspect the property?

Unfortunately not. Any travel expenses for joint properties need to be apportioned to each owner based on your respective percentages of ownership.

44 *Borrowing expenses*

Borrowing expenses in relation to organising a loan to purchase a rental property are tax deductions. But you can't claim them all in the first year that they are incurred, unless they are $100 or less. If your total deductible expenses are more than $100, the deduction you claim for those expenses must be spread over five years or the term of the loan, whichever is less.

Tax fact

If you obtained the loan part way through the income year, the deduction for the first year will be apportioned according to the number of days in the year that you had the loan.

The types of borrowing expenses you can claim as income tax deductions include the following:

▶ costs for preparing and filing mortgage documents

▶ lender's mortgage insurance

▶ loan establishment fees

▶ mortgage broker fees

▶ stamp duty charged on your mortgage

▶ title search fees charged by your lender

▶ valuation fees required for loan approval.

Mortgage discharge expenses, including those ridiculously high penalty interest costs involved in discharging a fixed-rate mortgage, are deductible in the year they are incurred to the extent that you took out the mortgage as security for the repayment of money you borrowed to use to produce assessable income.

💣 Pitfall

The following cannot be claimed as borrowing expenses:

▶ stamp duty charged by your state/territory government on the transfer (purchase) of the property title—this stamp duty can be included in calculating the 'cost base' of your property for CGT purposes

▶ insurance premiums where under the policy your loan will be paid out in the event that you die or become disabled or unemployed (this is a private expense)

▶ borrowing expenses on the portion of the loan you use for private purposes (for example, money used to buy a boat).

Tip

Stamp duty, preparation and registration costs you incur on the lease of an Australian Capital Territory (ACT) property are deductible to the extent that you use the property as a rental property. This is because freehold title cannot be obtained for properties in the ACT. They are commonly acquired under a 99-year Crown lease.

Example

On 16 September 2015, Robert took out a 30-year loan of $450 000 to purchase a rental property. Robert's deductible expenses were:

▶ $950 stamp duty on the mortgage
▶ $650 loan establishment fees
▶ $250 valuation fees required for loan.

Robert also paid $9200 stamp duty on the transfer of the property title for which he cannot claim a tax deduction. However, this expense will form part of the 'cost base'.

Robert would work out the borrowing expense deduction for each year as follows:

Borrowing expenses × number of relevant days in year ÷ number of days in 5 years = deduction for year

2015–16 (289 days) = $1850 × 289 ÷ 1826 = $293

2016–17 (365 days) = $1850 × 365 ÷ 1826 = $370

2017–18 (365 days) = $1850 × 365 ÷ 1826 = $370

2018–19 (365 days) = $1850 × 365 ÷ 1826 = $370

2019–20 (366 days) = $1850 × 366 ÷ 1826 = $371

2020–21 (76 days) = $1850 × 76 ÷ 1826 = $76

Source: © Australian Taxation Office for the Commonwealth of Australia.

> ☀ **Tip**
>
> If you repay your loan early and in fewer than five years, you can claim a deduction for the balance of the borrowing expenses in the year of repayment.

 ## Legal expenses

Like borrowing expenses, some legal expenses associated with rental properties are deductible and some are capital in nature and not deductible.

The types of legal expenses you can claim as income tax deductions include:

▶ preparing a lease agreement with your tenant

▶ evicting a non-paying tenant.

> 💣 **Pitfall**
>
> Most legal expenses are not deductible as they are of a capital nature. These include costs:
>
> ▶ for the preparation of loan documents (can be claimed as borrowing expenses)
> ▶ for the purchase (or sale) of your property
> ▶ associated with resisting land resumption
> ▶ associated with defending your title to the property.

Non-deductible legal expenses that are capital in nature may form part of the cost base of your property for CGT purposes (for more information, see p. 134).

Example

Luke purchased a rental property for $425 000. The expenses Luke paid that he can claim as a deduction on his next tax return were:

▶ $350 solicitor's fees for preparation of the lease
▶ $950 solicitor's fees for preparation of loan documents
▶ $850 stamp duty on the mortgage.

The deductions for the $950 solicitor's fees for handling the loan documents and the $850 stamp duty on the mortgage are considered borrowing expenses and must be claimed over five years, or the term of the loan, whichever is shorter.

The legal expenses that Luke paid for that he cannot claim as a deduction (capital costs that may form part of the cost base of the property) were:

▶ $1125 solicitor's fees for purchase of the property
▶ $13 450 stamp duty on the transfer of the property
▶ $60 title search fees.

Source: Australian Taxation Office.

46 *Other rental property deductions*

You may be entitled to claim an immediate deduction on these other property expenses in the income year you incur the expense:

▶ advertising for tenants
▶ bank charges

- body corporate fees and charges, also known as strata levies
- cleaning
- council rates
- electricity and gas
- gardening and lawnmowing
- in-house audio/video service charges
- insurance (building, contents and public liability)
- land tax
- letting fees
- pest control
- property agent's fees and commission
- quantity surveyor's fees
- secretarial and bookkeeping fees
- security patrol fees
- servicing costs — for example, servicing a water heater
- stationery and postage
- tax-related expenses
- telephone calls and rental
- water rates.

You can claim a deduction for these expenses only if you actually incur them and they are not paid by the tenant.

Land tax is a state tax imposed by each Australian state and territory (except the Northern Territory) and, as you might expect, each state has a different set of rules including different rates, thresholds and due dates. It is calculated on the unimproved value of the land (rather than the whole property value).

The tax is generally levied on the owners of land at midnight on 31 December of each year in NSW and Victoria (and 30 June for most other states) for land values greater than the threshold level, which are outlined in table 4.3. If you are liable for land tax you need to submit a land tax return. Owner-occupied homes or land used for primary production are generally exempt from land tax while properties held in a trust or company generally have a zero threshold.

 Tip

While it may not be tax deductible, take out basic life insurance that will cover your mortgage so that you have peace of mind knowing that your loved ones are not forced to sell when you (and your income) are no longer around.

Table 4.3: state land tax thresholds

State	Land tax threshold	Website
ACT	$75 000	www.revenue.act.gov.au
NSW	$432 000	www.osr.nsw.gov.au
Qld	$600 000	www.osr.qld.gov.au
SA	$316 000	www.revenuesa.sa.gov.au
Tas.	$25 000	www.sro.tas.gov.au
Vic.	$250 000	www.sro.vic.gov.au
WA	$300 000	www.osr.wa.gov.au

You can claim a deduction for certain expenses you incur for the period your property is rented or is available for rent. However, you cannot claim expenses of a capital nature or private nature—although you may be able to claim decline-in-value deductions or capital works deductions for certain capital expenses or include certain capital costs in the cost base of the property for CGT purposes.

 Pitfall

Expenses for which the ATO will not allow you to claim include:

▶ acquisition and disposal costs of the property

▶ body corporate payments to a special-purpose fund to pay for particular capital expenditure

▶ expenses you do not actually incur, such as water or electricity charges paid by your tenants

▶ expenses that are not related to the rental of a property, such as expenses connected to your own use of a holiday home that you rent out for part of the year.

:ᗄᐸ᎐ **Tip**

Make sure you have receipts to justify the deductions you are claiming, and can justify the connection between the expense and deriving the rental income (for example, it wasn't also for a private purpose).

 FAQ

I am thinking about letting out a room for a night here and there to travellers via one of those online sites such as Airbnb. Would I need to declare the money received as income? What are the implications, if any, if I don't declare it?

The tax rules are pretty clear. Any rental income that you receive — no matter how small — needs to be declared as assessable income in your return and you'll need to pay tax on it.

(continued)

FAQ *(cont'd)*

Trying to dodge the tax office by not declaring the income will end in tears. You may think that the income is so little that the ATO won't bother, but the cash economy is huge and is definitely on the tax man's hit list. Something like this is advertised on the net so the ATO is more likely to find out about it. Guests are paying electronically, which makes it easier to track down. I should also warn that people renting rooms in their home also need to be aware it's probably opening them up to capital gains tax when they sell their homes down the track.

47 *Foreign investment properties*

Australian tax residents have always been required to pay tax on their worldwide income. This includes declaring income earned from an overseas property that you may own in your Australian income tax return—even if it has been, or will be, taxed outside Australia.

Tax fact

If you have paid foreign tax in another country on that income, you may be entitled to an Australian foreign income tax offset, which provides relief from double taxation.

You can also claim the deductions (such as interest, repairs, depreciation, rates and insurance) as mentioned in tips 39–46 for a foreign rental property.

If your overseas property tax deductions are greater than your overseas rental income, you will have a foreign income loss. For many years, these foreign losses were quarantined and had to be carried forward to future years and only be offset against future foreign income.

However, many foreign property investors are not aware of the change in the rules a few years ago. Since 1 July 2008, foreign losses have not been quarantined from domestic income. This means that you can now 'negatively gear' your foreign income loss to reduce your Australian income.

Tax fact

Foreign losses incurred prior to the 2008–09 financial year can be claimed, subject to certain restrictions, in subsequent years. The transitional rules require the extinguishment of certain foreign losses on conversion and impose an annual limit on using the remaining losses for the first four years of the measure. A taxpayer may disregard the deduction limit in these years if they have $10 000 or less in pre-existing foreign losses or choose to utilise only $10 000 of these losses.

If you have incurred foreign rental property losses but did not declare them in your tax returns previously, send a letter to the ATO requesting that they issue amended assessments for those years.

Before you calculate your net income, all foreign income, deductions and foreign tax paid must be converted to Australian dollars. There are two ways of doing this. Depending on your circumstances, you can use:

▶ the exchange rates prevailing at specific times (generally used for specific transactions such as monthly rent, asset purchases and one-off expenses such as rates and insurance)

▶ an average exchange rate (generally used for expenses incurred over a period such as loan interest).

Pitfall

Australian residents are generally taxed on any capital gains made on overseas property and must declare the gain in their income tax return. If the gain is taxable in Australia and you have paid foreign tax on it, you may be entitled to a foreign income tax offset.

If an ATO audit detects that you did not declare offshore income there will be penalties and potentially a jail sentence if it was found to be an 'intentionally fraudulent act'.

 Capital gains tax

Careful tax planning is required by property investors when they intend to sell properties acquired after 19 September 1985, as the profit realised may be subject to capital gains tax (CGT). Capital gains are added to an individual's taxable income and taxed at their marginal tax rates.

☼ **Tip**

The simplest way to reduce CGT is to hold on to the investment for more than 12 months. Since 21 September 1999, investors have been entitled to claim a 50 per cent discount on capital gains they make on assets held for longer than a year. Since 8 May 2012, non-residents are no longer eligible for this discount on taxable Australian property.

Pitfall

Generally, an investment property owned for at least 12 months and then sold is entitled to 50 per cent discount on the capital gain. However, if your intention was to renovate and sell at a profit, rather than maintain the property as a long-term, income-producing investment, you may be taxed on the entire profit as a 'profit-making scheme'.

You will make a capital gain from the sale of your rental property to the extent that the capital proceeds you receive are more than the cost base of the property. The cost base of a property includes:

▶ the original purchase price

▶ incidental costs associated with acquiring the property — such as legal fees and stamp duty

▶ incidental costs associated with disposing of the property — such as legal fees and real estate agent's commissions

▶ improvements made to the property (less any depreciation previously claimed).

 Tip

If you are thinking of selling a profitable asset, such as shares or property, it may be worth deferring the sale exchange until after the end of the financial year. By doing so, you will get an extra year to pay any CGT liability and earn an extra year's interest until you eventually pay it.

CGT is payable in the year that you exchange, rather than the year that you settle, so make sure you exchange on a property after 1 July.

As discussed earlier, negative gearing is generally a good strategy for high-income earners as they get bigger refunds than lower income earners. Unfortunately it has the opposite effect when a property is sold and subject to CGT.

Tip

A good strategy is to delay selling your investment property until a year when your income will be lower and you will fall into a lower marginal tax bracket. This is particularly relevant when investors are nearing retirement as they should consider delaying any CGT liability until they have retired and earn little or no income.

Tax fact

You can use your capital losses to offset the capital gains you make on other assets.

While a person's principal place of residence is CGT-free when they sell it, it is possible to move out of the property, rent it and still claim this exemption for up to six years. After that time, the CGT clock is no longer frozen and starts ticking.

Bonus resources

For more information about CGT, the ATO has the excellent *Personal investors guide to capital gains tax* (NAT 4152).

FAQ

If we move into the granny flat in the back of our property and rent out the main house, are we subject to capital gains tax?

When you move into your granny flat, it will be treated as a separate asset for CGT purposes. You will need to consider which asset to claim the principal place of residence exemption — ideally the property with the greatest opportunity for growth, which will probably be the main house. Of course, any periods that you live in both places at the same time are exempt from CGT.

49 *PAYG withholding variation*

As mentioned earlier, one of the major downsides to negative gearing is cash flow.

My preference is that you wait until the end of the year to get your refund as it is a forced form of saving. But if cash flow is tight, you may want to complete a pay-as-you-go (PAYG) withholding variation application, which reduces the tax from your monthly pay. The form is virtually a mini-tax return, which estimates your taxable income. You still need to lodge an annual tax return.

Example

Jason is on the highest marginal tax rate. In the year ending 30 June 2017 he expects to incur a net rental loss of $20 000. Instead of waiting to lodge his 2016–17 tax return in July 2017 and getting a refund of $9800, he can submit a PAYG withholding variation application with the ATO in May 2016. As a result, Jason has $816.67 less PAYG tax withheld from his salary each month to help him meet his mortgage commitments instead of waiting until the end of the financial year.

 Tip

The rate of withholding will hopefully match your year-end tax liability. If you underestimate your income then expect to have a tax shortfall, which isn't desirable. Instead, make sure you give yourself a buffer by not being too aggressive with estimating deductions.

If your circumstances change after your PAYG variation is approved (perhaps you increased the rent, your expenses are lower than expected or you sold your property), then submit a new PAYG variation straight away. Otherwise you may have an unwanted tax liability at the end of the year.

You can lodge your application in a paper form or electronically over the internet. The varied rate of withholding will start from the next payday after your pay office receives the notice of withholding variation approval from the ATO.

Tax fact

PAYG withholding variations are not solely available to taxpayers who are negatively gearing rental properties. They can also be used for other purposes where a taxpayer's assessable income is substantially reduced for tax-deductible expenditure such as work-related car expenses, self-education costs or margin-loan interest.

Your variation generally finishes on 30 June each year so you need to do a new PAYG withholding variation application each year — they do not roll forward. To continue to have reduced tax withheld after this date, you must lodge another PAYG withholding variation application — at least six weeks before; that is, by 15 May each year.

Pitfall

Anyone using the withholding variation strategy to help with cash flow needs to be disciplined enough to use the extra money to meet the shortfall, rather than using it for everyday living expenses.

Remember, if you apply for advanced refunds in this way, there will be no end-of-year tax deduction and no 'forced form of saving'.

50 *Property genuinely available for rent*

As we have seen, deductions for investment properties can be quite substantial and generate large tax refunds, particularly if a property doesn't generate much rent by comparison. However, the property must be rented, or 'genuinely available' for rental, in the income year for which you claim a deduction. If you start to use the property for private purposes, you cannot claim any interest expenses you incur after you start using the property for private purposes.

 Tip

It is very important that you have a clear intention of renting your property. If you make no attempt to advertise your property or set the rent unrealistically high, the ATO will find that you have no intention of renting your property and your rental claims may not be allowed.

In some situations, rental expenses may need to be apportioned. For example, if your holiday home is used by you, your friends or your relatives free of charge for part of the year, you are not entitled to a deduction for costs incurred during those periods.

Tax fact

If you rent your property to family or friends at below market rent, the ATO may treat this as a 'private' arrangement and only allow you to claim sufficient deductions to offset the rent, but not enough to make a tax loss.

● Pitfall

Be careful not to overstate interest deductions where the loan is partly for private purposes, such as claiming interest on a holiday house property where it is used, say for one month (one-twelfth), by your family for holidays.

Part V

Your shares

Owning shares can bring about some important tax considerations for shareholders.

Share ownership in Australia increased substantially in the 1990s following the privatisation of a number of government-owned enterprises (such as Telstra and the Commonwealth Bank) and the demutualisation of many financial service providers (such as AMP, MBF, NRMA and NIB).

And for the majority of Australians the complexity of tax returns increased substantially as a result, with the advent of dividends, franking credits, share buybacks, rights issues, margin loans, capital gains tax and the like.

Tax fact

If you hold shares, the ATO requires you to keep proper records for tax purposes, including:

► 'buy' and 'sell' contracts for five years from the date you dispose of your shares
► dividend statements for five years from the date you lodge your tax return.

In part V, I will focus on the tax implications of owning a share portfolio as well as looking at ways to minimise any CGT liability in the future.

Pitfall

Don't try to hide your income on shares from the ATO. The tax man has improved his data-matching capabilities in recent years by gaining access to information from the ASX and various share registries on dividends and share disposals by taxpayers.

Bonus resources

For more information about tax and shares, the ATO has an excellent publication called *You and your shares 2012* (NAT 2632).

Dividends

Being a shareholder entitles you to a share of a company's profits that are usually paid as dividends. In Australia, there are two types of dividends that are assessable for tax purposes:

▶ franked dividends

▶ unfranked dividends.

💣 **Pitfall**

According to the ATO, if a private company lends money to a shareholder (or associate) and the loan is not fully repaid before the end of the income year, the outstanding amount may be treated as a non-commercial loan and assessed as an unfranked dividend in the shareholder's tax return to the extent of the private company's retained earnings.

Franked dividends are dividends paid by Australian companies from profits that have been taxed previously. A dividend which carries tax credits for the whole dividend is known as a fully franked dividend.

Unfranked dividends are dividends paid by Australian companies from profits that have not had any company tax paid on them.

 Tip

Bank charges and any interest payments on funds borrowed to acquire shares are generally tax deductible.

Tax fact

Franked dividends paid to non-resident individuals are exempt from Australian income tax. However, they are not entitled to any franking tax offset for franked dividends.

Any unfranked dividends paid to a non-resident are subject to a final withholding tax, generally 15 per cent if Australia has a double taxation agreement with the taxpayer's resident country, otherwise at 30 per cent.

When an Australian company pays you a dividend, it must also send you a statement advising:

▶ the amount of the dividend that is unfranked

▶ the amount of the dividend that is franked

▶ any franking credits

▶ any TFN withholding tax withheld on unfranked dividends.

 Tip

Make sure you quote your TFN to any company that pays you a dividend, otherwise withholding tax at the highest marginal rate (47 per cent) will be deducted on any unfranked dividends paid to you. If you have TFN tax withheld you must include it in your tax return so that you receive the credit in your assessment.

Example

This is an example of what a dividend statement would look like:

ABC Limited

ABN 12 345 678 901

Shareholder dividend statement

Payment date 15 February 2016

Notification of 2015 final dividend — paid 15 February 2016

Security description	No. of shares	Unfranked amount	Franked amount	Franking credit
Ordinary shares	18 000	$500	$700	$300
TFN amount	$0.00			
Net dividend	$1200.00			

Please note that your tax file number has been received and recorded.

Please retain this advice for taxation purposes.

Please advise promptly in writing of any change of address.

Source: © Australian Taxation Office for the Commonwealth of Australia.

 Tip

Taxpayers regularly get the timing of the dividend payments wrong. Only dividends paid between 1 July and 30 June the following year should be included in your return. Confusion usually occurs when a final dividend is paid in July or August yet the dividend statement says that it is in respect of the year ended 30 June. In this instance the dividend should be declared in the following tax year.

> **Tax fact**
>
> If you had any shares in joint names, you are not required to lodge a separate partnership tax return. Simply show your proportion of any dividends paid in your individual tax return.

52 *Franking credits*

Franking credits, also known as imputation credits, were introduced in 1985 to prevent the double taxation of dividends to individual shareholders after companies had already paid tax on the profits distributed.

Franking credits are amounts of tax paid by the company that are allocated to your franked dividend. There is no franking credit associated with an unfranked dividend.

> **Tax fact**
>
> Dividends paid to shareholders by Australian companies are taxed under an 'imputation' system where tax paid by a company may be imputed to shareholders. Any tax paid by the company is allocated by way of franking credits attached to the dividends paid to shareholders.

The amount of the franking credit is calculated as follows:

Franking credit = franked dividend paid × company tax rate ÷ (100% − company tax rate)

Despite small companies enjoying a lower rate from 1 July 2015, dividends from all companies should apply the standard 30 per cent company tax rate when calculating the franking credit as follows:

$$\text{Franking credit} = \text{franked dividend} \times 30 \div 70$$

Example

On 15 February 2016 an Australian resident company, ABC Ltd, paid Peter, a resident individual, a fully franked dividend of $700 and an unfranked dividend of $500.

Peter's assessable income for 2015–16 in respect of the dividend is:

Unfranked dividend	$500
Franked dividend	$700
Franking credit ($700 × 30 ÷ 70)	$300
Total assessable dividends	**$1500**

The franking credit is included in the definition of assessable income and must also be declared in your income tax return. Tax is payable at your applicable tax rate on these amounts but the franking credit becomes a tax offset against any tax payable.

 Tip

When you are looking to buy shares, have a look at the ones that pay fully franked dividends as they provide a 30 per cent credit for company tax already paid. If you earn less than $80 000 you effectively get dividends tax-free, which isn't a bad thing.

Apart from disclosing it as income, there is no requirement to claim the tax offset in your tax return. The ATO will automatically put it on your notice of assessment. The offset can be used to reduce any liability from all forms of income and from net taxable capital gains.

Example

Using the dividend from the previous example, Peter's tax payable following the dividend is calculated as follows:

Total assessable dividends	$1500
Other assessable income	$78 500
Taxable income	**$80 000**
Tax on taxable income	$17 547
Add: Medicare levy (2%)	$1600
Less: Franking tax offset	($300)
Net tax payable	**$18 847**

 Tip

Companies that pay fully franked dividends provide a better yield after tax than those that pay unfranked dividends because you get a credit for the 30 per cent income tax already paid.

 Pitfall

You may not be eligible for the franking tax offset unless you continuously hold shares 'at risk' for at least 45 days (90 days for preference shares) around, and including, the ex-dividend date. This is known as the '45 day holding period' rule. However, under the small shareholder exemption, this rule does not apply if your total franking credit entitlement is below $5000, which is roughly equivalent to receiving a fully franked dividend of $11 666 (based on the current tax rate of 30 per cent for companies).

Individuals who have franking credits greater than any tax payable do not lose them but get them refunded instead.

Bonus resources

If you are eligible to claim a franking tax offset for 2015–16 but you are not otherwise required to lodge a tax return, you should complete the form *Application for a refund of franking credits for individuals* (NAT 4098).

53 *Dividend reinvestment plans*

Not all dividends are paid in cash. If it is a private company they can be credited against the shareholder's loan account. Or you can be issued with new shares in lieu of the dividend via a 'dividend reinvestment plan' (DRP) or scheme.

Any dividend used to acquire shares under the DRP forms part of your Australian taxable income and you are required to pay tax on these reinvested dividends.

💣 Pitfall

A lot of people think that because they didn't receive a dividend in cash, but rather received some more shares in the company via a DRP, the dividend is not taxable. This is incorrect. All dividends paid, whether in cash or shares, must be included in your assessable income in the year they are received.

You are also subject to tax on any capital gain made when you dispose of shares you have received under a DRP. For the purpose of calculating any capital gain or loss, the cost of the shares acquired under a DRP is taken as the market price on the date of the dividend as shown on the statement.

 Tip

Keep a record of all reinvested dividends to help you work out any capital gains or losses you make when you dispose of shares. The cost base must be the same as the amount that you previously declared as a dividend.

Tax fact

In addition to DRPs, shareholders may receive bonus shares in a company from time to time which are extra shares received based on your existing shareholding. They are not taxable on receipt but if you dispose of any bonus shares received after 19 September 1985 you may have to:

▶ pay tax on any capital gain
▶ average out the cost base of your existing shares in the company.

 ## *Lower income earners*

There can be some significant benefits in holding shares in the name of the spouse who is on the lower income, because any dividends (and capital gains) are taxed at a lower rate.

The marginal income tax rates for resident individuals for the 2015–16 financial year are shown in table 5.1.

Table 5.1: tax rates for individuals excluding levies (2015–16)

Taxable income	Tax on this income
0–$18 200	Nil
$18 201–$37 000	19c for each $1 over $18 200
$37 001–$80 000	$3572 plus 32.5c for each $1 over $37 000
$80 001–$180 000	$17 547 plus 37c for each $1 over $80 000
$180 001 and over	$54 547 plus 45c for each $1 over $180 000

Source: © Australian Taxation Office for the Commonwealth of Australia.

 Tip

For those earning less than $80 000, franked dividends are effectively tax-free because they get a credit for the 30 per cent company tax already paid—the equivalent of the marginal rate at that level.

For those on lower marginal tax rates (that is, earning less than $37 000), the excess franking tax offsets can be used to reduce your tax liability from other forms of income, including net taxable capital gains, or can even be refunded.

Example

Tom earns $310 000 while his wife Suzie earns $20 000. They just sold their house and are considering purchasing a share portfolio of stocks in blue-chip companies. As Suzie has a marginal tax rate of 21 per cent (including the 2 per cent Medicare levy), it is more beneficial for her to own the portfolio in her name than for Tom to own it, as he is on the highest tax bracket of 49 per cent.

(continued)

Example *(cont'd)*

The tax savings on a share portfolio in Suzie's name that generates an annual income stream of franked dividends of, say, $20 000 would be as much as $6437, or 32.2 per cent of the income received.

 Pitfall

A share portfolio in the low-income-earning spouse's name may have an impact on any government benefits being received, as dividend income and capital gains are included under the income test and the share portfolio itself is assessed by Centrelink under its assets test.

If there are some significant capital gains in a portfolio, then they may push the low-income earner into a higher tax bracket, thus negating some of the tax benefits that may be received. In this instance it may be an idea to spread the disposal over a few income years.

There is also a need to look into a crystal ball and forecast what income levels will be for spouses in future years, especially if the current income is abnormally low, and that events such as returning to work after the kids go back to school are fully considered prior to making any purchase.

Example

If, in two years' time, Suzie gets a full-time job with a salary of $180 000 and Tom decides to reduce the number of days he works and only earns $60 000 per annum, there is no longer any benefit in having the share portfolio in Suzie's name as she is now on a high tax bracket of 47 per cent while Tom only pays 34.5 per cent.

While it is possible to transfer shares across to the other partner's name in an off-market transfer, such an event would trigger CGT, which might negate any benefit gained by such a switch.

 Tip

Senior Australians are not required to pay any income tax if their income is below $33 044 for singles (or $29 739 each if a couple). As a result, notwithstanding the risks associated with share-price fluctuations, an investment strategy of having a share portfolio that generates fully franked dividends (and franking credits subsequently refunded) may be quite lucrative for those eligible for the senior and pensioner tax offset.

55 *Borrowing to buy shares*

A common, yet risky, investment strategy used by share investors has been to borrow money, usually via a margin loan, to buy shares.

 Pitfall

Borrowing is a good strategy in a rising market, but it can multiply any losses in a falling market. The last thing you want is a loan to repay but no shares to show for it. Don't consider borrowing if you are new to investing.

Just like the tax rules for investment properties, if you borrow money to buy a share portfolio, you can claim a tax deduction for the loan interest, provided it is reasonable to expect that assessable income (dividends or capital gains) will be derived from the share investment. If the loan has a private component, you will only be able to claim interest incurred on the part of the loan used to acquire the shares.

The benefit of such a strategy is that the interest expense should offset any dividend income received, resulting in franking credits that can be offset against other taxable income. Hopefully the shares increase in value under this strategy and any capital gains are only realised in a later year when the taxpayer is on a lower tax rate, for example, in retirement.

 Tip

If you expect to earn a lower income next tax year (for example, due to redundancy or maternity leave), an excellent strategy to consider is prepaying interest 12 months in advance before year end on your margin loan to maximise your tax deduction based on the higher marginal tax rate.

Borrowing expenses (such as establishment fees, legal expenses and stamp duty on loans) may be claimed for tax purposes. If borrowing expenses are more than $100, then they must be apportioned over five years or over the term of the loan, whichever is less. Borrowing expenses under $100 are fully deductible in the year incurred.

 Pitfall

For a borrowing strategy to work you need to get a return greater than the cost of the interest rate that you are paying (which is generally at a premium for margin loans), otherwise you are falling further behind despite receiving the tax benefits. Remember the ABC motto: Absolute Bloody Cash!

Some investors use a capital-protected borrowings strategy, where shares are bought using a borrowing arrangement where the borrower is wholly or partly protected against a fall in the market value of the investments.

Tax fact

Any interest paid for capital protection under a capital-protected borrowing arrangement for shares is not deductible but instead is treated as if it were a payment for a put option.

Pitfall

While there was a change in the law in September 2007 that made it possible to borrow within self managed super funds, special rules apply. Seek professional advice on how to structure this to avoid any contravention of the complex superannuation rules.

FAQ

Is it possible to claim the interest charged on money borrowed to purchase shares when there were no dividends paid in that tax year?

Yes most definitely. So long as it is reasonable to expect some assessable income from this share investment over time, be it dividends or capital gains, then you can claim a deduction for loan interest in the tax year in which it is incurred, whether or not you receive income in the same year.

Other allowable deductions

The following are examples of deductions that you may be able to claim for costs incurred in deriving income from shares.

Ongoing management fees

Ongoing management fees are allowable deductions, but only a proportion of the fee is deductible if the advice covers non-investment matters or is related to investments that do not produce assessable income.

> **💣 Pitfall**
>
> Any cost for drawing up an initial investment plan is not tax-deductible.

Travel expenses

Travel expenses incurred to visit a stockbroker or annual general meeting are fully tax-deductible to the extent that the sole purpose of the travel relates to the share investment. If the travel is predominantly of a private nature, such as a holiday, only the expenses that relate directly to servicing your portfolio will be allowable as a tax deduction.

Journals and publications

Specialist investment journals and publications, subscriptions or sharemarket information services you use to manage your share portfolio can be claimed against your investment income.

Internet access

If you use the internet to manage your portfolio—such as buying and selling shares online—the cost of internet access will be deductible to the extent that the internet is used for this purpose. Any private usage is not claimable and must be added back.

 Tip

You can claim depreciation on the proportion of the decline in value of your computer and printer based on the percentage of your total computer use that relates to managing your investments.

Other deductions

Any other expenses you incur that relate directly to maintaining your portfolio are also deductible, including:

▶ bookkeeping expenses

▶ telephone

▶ postage.

 Pitfall

The ATO outlines that, unless you are considered to be a share trader, you cannot claim a deduction for brokerage and stamp duty on the acquisition of shares. These will form part of the cost base for CGT calculations when you eventually dispose of the shares.

57 Shares and capital gains tax

With a potential to go up to 49 per cent, CGT can have a hugely negative impact when calculating the net return on an investment. It is a tax imposed upon gains made from the disposal of assets, usually shares or investment properties, that were acquired after 19 September 1985. When a net capital gain arises it is included in your taxable income and is subject to income tax at the marginal tax rates.

> **Tax fact**
>
> CGT is included in your annual income tax return; however, assets acquired before 20 September 1985 are exempt from CGT.

You make a capital gain or loss when a 'CGT event' occurs. These events could be when you:

▶ sell your shares

▶ have your shares redeemed, cancelled, surrendered or considered valueless by a liquidator

▶ receive a payment (other than dividends) from a company as a shareholder

▶ give away your shares.

The capital gain is calculated on the difference between the proceeds that you receive from the sale of your shares and the amount you originally paid for them. Brokerage is included in your cost base.

Tip

The simplest way to reduce CGT is to hold on to the investment for more than 12 months. Since September 1999, a 50 per cent discount on capital gains is allowed for shares held for longer than a year.

 Pitfall

If you do try to wait for the 12 months' holding period to tick over, be careful that the sharemarket doesn't collapse during this time. A dramatic fall in share price could erase any tax benefit that the 50 per cent discount provides if you are not careful.

Shares sold back to a company under a buyback arrangement result in a capital gain or loss. Part of the buyback price may be treated as an assessable dividend for income tax purposes. If the buyback comes from a listed company, a class ruling is usually issued to assist shareholders with any tax implications.

Tax fact

To calculate any capital gain, the ATO requires you to keep proper records for tax purposes including:

▶ 'buy' and 'sell' contract notes, showing the date and amounts
▶ dividend statements for any dividend reinvestment schemes that you participated in.

The ATO will allow you to establish a CGT asset register (but only if it is in a certain format) if you do not want to keep your records, particularly if you hold shares for a long time. For more information, see the ATO's Taxation Ruling *TR 2002/10 Income tax: capital gains tax: asset register*.

Bonus resources

For more information about CGT, the ATO has the excellent *Personal investors guide to capital gains tax* (NAT 4152).

58 *Realising capital losses*

One of the best ways to reduce your CGT bill is to offset any gains that you have made during the financial year with any losses incurred on other share investments. It is important to note that the losses must be crystallised (or realised) in order for them to be offset against any capital gains made. If a loss remains unrealised (not sold) at the end of the financial year, you cannot claim it in your return until the year that you actually dispose of the investment.

Example

Peter makes a $6200 capital gain on the sale of BHP shares in July 2015. He also owns shares in another stock, XYZ, which he bought for $10 000 but which is now only worth $4000. If he realises this loss by selling these shares before 30 June 2016 he can reduce his taxable capital gain by $6000 to only $200. If Peter disposes of these XYZ shares after 1 July 2016, then he must pay tax on the whole $6200 gain.

It is good tax-planning practice to see if there is an opportunity to reduce the tax on gains made earlier in the year by selling a few non-performing shares. This is particularly relevant if the sharemarket is performing like a roller-coaster and there is a slump after a big rise earlier in the year.

Tip

Maintain an Excel spreadsheet (sample available on my website www.mrtaxman.com.au) to keep track of the cost base and market value of your share portfolio on a stock-by-stock basis. This will assist with the tax-planning process to help determine which stocks could be sold to offset capital gains already made during the year.

Obviously, if you haven't made any gains in the year then there is no need to crystallise any losses that you are currently carrying in your share portfolio.

Tip

Realised capital losses can be carried forward indefinitely until they are fully utilised. Check your past tax returns for any available from previous years.

While you could purchase back your shares that have been realised for the loss, it is not advisable. Although yet to be challenged in the courts, the ATO has warned that the practice of 'wash sales' (where you sell shares and buy them back straight away for the purposes of realising capital losses to offset against other capital gains) could be considered an avoidance of income tax under Part IVA of the tax legislation. This comes with some hefty tax penalties.

If you are considering such a scenario, ensure that you purchase a different number of shares from the number that you originally sold. Or if your portfolio simply needs to be rebalanced in a particular industry, then buy a similar stock instead. For example, if you sell your Westpac Bank shares to crystallise a capital loss, buy a different bank stock such as ANZ or Commonwealth Bank instead as a replacement.

Also note that capital losses must be applied against capital gains prior to any 50 per cent discount being applied to shares held for more than 12 months.

Example

Natalie has a $500 discounted capital gain based on a raw capital gain of $1000 from ABC shares held more than 12 months. She also incurred a $700 capital loss from the disposal of XYZ shares. She must offset the capital loss of $700 against the $1000 raw capital gain, before applying the 50 per cent discount on the remaining $300 gain. As a result she will need to pay tax on the $150 discounted net capital gain.

59 *Inheriting share portfolios*

If you receive shares from a deceased estate you need to be aware of some consequences for tax. Future dividends received are treated as normal income. The only variation is if a child under 18 receives income via a testamentary trust — then it is taxed at adult rates instead of the high rates imposed on minors.

While normal CGT rules apply if a beneficiary sells an asset they have inherited, there are a few variances depending on when they inherited the shares and when they were originally purchased by the deceased.

All inherited shares are considered to have been acquired for CGT purposes on the day that the person died. If that was before 20 September 1985, you disregard any capital gain or loss made from the asset.

If the shares were originally acquired before 20 September 1985, your cost base is the market value of the asset on the day the person died.

 Pitfall

According to the ATO, if the shares were originally acquired by the deceased before 20 September 1985, you must use the market value on the day the person died, not the market value on the day you received the shares.

Tax fact

While death can be sudden, it may be possible to do some tax planning before someone dies:

▶ Use any capital losses that are accumulated or unrealised prior to death, as these cannot be passed on to beneficiaries.

▶ Bequeath share portfolios to beneficiaries on lower taxable incomes so that tax paid on income and capital gains in the future are minimal and the capital is preserved for as long as possible.

▶ If the estate is substantial and there are children under age 18 who are potential beneficiaries, consider establishing a testamentary trust so they can access the favourable adult marginal tax rates.

If a deceased person acquired their shares on or after 20 September 1985, your cost base is taken to be the deceased person's cost base of the shares on the day the person died. The indexation method can be used for capital gains purposes if the deceased person died before 21 September 1999.

> **Pitfall**
>
> If the deceased person died after 20 September 1999, the ATO does not allow you to use the indexation method.

> **!**
>
> **Tax fact**
>
> Often family members give shares to relatives while they are still alive; for example, a parent gives shares to their child. If you receive shares as a gift, the market value on the date that you received them will be your cost base for CGT purposes.

60   *Share traders versus share investors*

The distinction between share traders and share investors is significant for tax purposes as you deal with gains and losses differently.

The ATO will consider you to be a share trader if you conduct your business activities for the sole purpose of earning income from the buying and selling of shares. Losses incurred are treated the same as any other losses from business — provided the non-commercial losses rules are satisfied, an immediate deduction is available against other taxable income.

> **Tax fact**
>
> In financial years when shares plummet, it is quite common for taxpayers to try to class themselves as share traders.

> **Tax fact**
>
> To be classed as a share trader, the ATO may ask you to prove you are carrying on a share trading business, including providing evidence that shows:
>
> ▶ the purchase and sale of shares on a regular basis
> ▶ the use of any share trading techniques
> ▶ decisions based on thorough analysis of relevant market information
> ▶ a contingency plan in the event of a major market shift
> ▶ a trading plan showing analysis and research of each potential investment and the market, and any formula for deciding when to hold or sell investments.

The ATO will consider you to be a share investor if you:

▶ invest in shares with the sole intention of earning income from dividends and capital growth

▶ are eligible for the 50 per cent CGT discount on gain

▶ claim losses incurred as a capital loss and not as an immediate deduction

▶ carry forward capital losses to be offset against future capital gains.

Tax fact

In financial years when shares rocket up, it is quite common for taxpayers to try to class themselves as share investors so they can get the 50 per cent CGT discount on gains made for shares held for more than 12 months.

How you treat your investment activities in prior tax returns is the main factor in determining the correct way to deal with losses in the current tax year. If there has been little or no change in your investment activity, you should treat the investments in the same manner again in the current year.

Example

George has been purchasing shares for a number of years for the purpose of earning income from dividends. In a previous year George sold shares and claimed the 50 per cent CGT discount. It is expected that George will claim any losses in the current year as capital losses.

If you change from being a share investor to being a share trader (or vice versa) the ATO may request evidence that proves the change is accurate and that you have not declared your income incorrectly in previous tax returns.

> **💣 Pitfall**
>
> The ATO has issued a warning to taxpayers who seek to change their status from that of a share investor to a share trader. For more information, see *Taxpayer Alert 2009/12*.
>
> If an ATO audit finds that you have incorrectly claimed trading losses and you are unable to satisfactorily show that you are carrying on an investment business, your deduction will be disallowed and penalties may apply.

61 *Rights and options*

Companies sometimes issue their shareholders with rights or options to purchase additional shares.

A 'one-for-ten' rights issue means that shareholders are entitled to purchase an additional share for every 10 shares that they own. The right can be exercised, sold on the stock exchange or simply allowed to lapse.

> **❗ Tax fact**
>
> If you receive rights, the ATO will not require you to include them in your assessable income provided:
>
> ▶ you already own shares in the company and the rights were issued to you because of this ownership
>
> ▶ your shares, and the rights, were not traditional securities or convertible interests, or were being treated as revenue assets or trading stock at the time they were issued
>
> ▶ the rights were not acquired under an employee share scheme.

Where the above criteria are satisfied then the only tax consequences that may arise with rights issues involve CGT. In other situations, rights issues may result in having to disclose assessable income in your tax return.

If you are issued a right to sell your shares (that is, a put), then the market value of the right should be included in your assessable income at the time of issue and will form part of your cost base for the rights or shares, if you exercised the rights.

Companies may also issue their shareholders with options. If you receive an option, you have the right to acquire or sell shares in the company at a specified price on a specified date. These options can be traded on the stock exchange or allowed to lapse.

Tax fact

Options are similar to rights except that they are normally held for a longer period than rights before they lapse or must be exercised. According to the ATO, options can be issued to both existing shareholders and non-shareholders while rights can only be issued initially to existing shareholders.

Exchange-traded options are types of options that are not created by the company but by independent third parties and are traded on the stock exchange. Option trading will generally be considered a business activity and subject to the normal business income rules.

Pitfall

Option trading is the quickest way to make money, but it is also the quickest way to lose money. I have seen more people lose money on options than make money on them.

Employee share schemes

Some companies give employees the chance to participate in employee share schemes (ESS) by offering ESS interests such as shares, rights or options to be acquired at a discount, which are then subject to tax. ESS interests can be taxed under the employee share scheme rules as well as being subsequently taxed under the CGT regime.

> **! Tax fact**
>
> For tax purposes the ATO requires you to keep a record of:
>
> ► the dates, amounts and number of ESS interests that were acquired, exercised or sold
> ► the amount of the discount you received on the date of acquisition
> ► the ESS rules
> ► details of elections made to include discounts in the year of acquisition for interests acquired before 1 July 2009.

The tax rules for the different types of ESS are:

► Taxed upfront

   ☐ The discount you receive is assessable in the financial year you acquired the ESS interests.

   ☐ You are eligible for a $1000 reduction if your taxable income after adjustments is less than $180000 and you don't hold or control more than 5 per cent of the company.

   ☐ For CGT purposes, the interest is taken to have been acquired at market value on the day it was originally acquired.

► Tax deferred

☐ If you acquire less than $5000 of shares via salary sacrifice, or if there is a real risk of forfeiture, the tax on any discount is deferred until the 'deferred taxing point' occurs, usually seven years after you acquire the share/right or when you cease employment.

☐ The amount assessed will be the market value of the ESS interests at the deferred taxing point, reduced by the cost base.

☐ If you dispose of an ESS interest within 30 days after a deferred taxing point occurred, the date of that disposal becomes the deferred taxing point (known as the '30-day rule').

☐ For CGT purposes the interest is taken to have been reacquired immediately after the deferred taxing point in order to determine any eligibility for the 50 per cent CGT discount.

Tax fact

From 1 July 2015, options issued to employees of start-up companies — defined as those less than 10 years' old and with an annual turnover of less than $50 million — will be taxed when they are converted to shares (rather than at the time that the option is originally received). Employees who exercise these options after a minimum of three years will also get a 15 per cent tax deduction (with the Commissioner being allowed to exercise discretion in circumstances outside the employees' control that make the minimum three year holding period impossible to meet). It was proposed in the 2015–16 federal budget that where options are converted into shares and the resulting shares are sold within 12 months of exercise, the CGT discount concession will be available.

Tax fact

You should receive an ESS statement from your employer if you participated in an ESS in order to finalise your income tax return.

Example

Oliver works for XYZ Ltd and acquires 500 shares in XYZ under a taxed-upfront share scheme on 29 July 2015. The total market value of the shares is $5000. Oliver is required to pay $2800 to purchase the shares — thus acquiring the shares for a discount of $2200.

Oliver's adjusted taxable income (including the $2200 discount) is $71 000 so he is eligible for the upfront concession of $1000 in his 2015–16 tax return. For CGT purposes, his cost base is $5000.

Pitfall

When ESS interests are acquired by your spouse, you still need to include the discount in your own tax return but your spouse would be subject to any CGT in the future.

Share portfolios within self managed superannuation funds

Earlier in part V, we looked at the merits of having a share portfolio in a low-income earner's name and the taxes that can be saved as a result. There are similar benefits with having shares held by a self managed superannuation fund (SMSF).

Tip

Capital gains on share disposals are taxed at either 10 per cent or 15 per cent in a super fund, which is substantially lower than the 24.5 per cent or 49 per cent that you potentially could be taxed at if you held shares as an individual.

As super funds only pay a flat 15 per cent tax on their income, shares that pay fully franked dividends are quite attractive as imputation credits have a 30 per cent tax credit attached to them. This means that the imputation credit not only covers the tax on the dividend but can also be offset against other income earned by the fund.

Pitfall

There are a few limitations with having an SMSF, which we will discuss in more detail in part VI, but one of the biggest ones is that you can't access your funds until you satisfy the condition of release, which is usually reaching your preservation age in retirement.

In the accumulation stage, an SMSF pays tax at 15 per cent on its taxable income. Any capital gains on investments held for more than 12 months are taxed at only 10 per cent. This is substantially lower than the marginal tax rates for those taxpayers earning over $37 000. And once a pension is started, a fund pays no tax at all on its income or its capital gains.

 Tip

When an SMSF goes into a pension phase, it provides a special opportunity to avoid CGT altogether on a share portfolio as no tax is payable when shares are sold during this stage.

An investment strategy where there is a share portfolio generating predominantly franked dividend income is quite tax-friendly in an SMSF. The fund receives excess franking credits on the difference between the 30 per cent company tax attached to the dividends and its 15 per cent tax rate. The dividends are effectively tax-free and these excess credits can be used to reduce tax on other fund income.

SMSF members are allowed to transfer shares into the fund 'in-specie' unlike property. There are contribution limits as to the amount of shares that can be transferred at market value each year. Depending on the personal tax situation of the member, the transfer may be tax-deductible at the taxpayer's marginal tax rate but assessable to the fund at 15 per cent (increasing to 30 per cent for individuals with income greater than $300 000).

Tip

If you have a share portfolio in your own name and the sharemarket crashes, you have a great opportunity. If you are confident that the shares will bounce back, transfer the shares 'in-specie' into a lower taxed environment of an SMSF. The SMSF will potentially only pay 10 per cent tax on future gains and can use excess franking credits on other income under this strategy.

However, the 'in-specie transfer' will be considered a CGT event and will trigger the CGT provisions for the individual taxpayer. To limit any CGT it is preferable to transfer shares that have not incurred large gains or those that can be offset against other capital losses.

Part VI

Your superannuation

Superannuation is money set aside throughout your working life to provide for your retirement. Behind the family home, it's the second-largest asset for many Australians, maybe even the largest. But it is ridiculous how little attention is paid to it. You need to take the time to look after one of your biggest assets. It doesn't need much. If you don't have enough money in super to look after yourself when you retire there are government pensions to support you.

> **Tax fact**
>
> As at 31 December 2014, the total assets within Australian superannuation were $1.934 trillion (Australian Prudential Regulation Authority 2015b), which was greater than the market capitalisation

(continued)

> **Tax fact** *(cont'd)*
>
> of the Australian equities market of $1.575 trillion (Australian Securities Exchange 2015), the combined deposits on the books of all Australian banks of $1.796 trillion (Australian Prudential Regulation Authority 2015a) and the Gross Domestic Product of Australia of $1.593 trillion (Australian Bureau of Statistics 2015).

Figure 6.1 reports the movement in total assets held by the various segments of the Australian superannuation industry since 1996. Total assets in the industry have increased by 734 per cent from $245.5 billion to $1934.1 billion as at 31 December 2014, the number of funds rising almost fivefold from 105 377 in 1996 to 548 142 funds and the number of member accounts doubling during the period to approximately 32 million (Australian Prudential Regulation Authority 2015b). The economic significance of the superannuation industry in Australia, measured by assets in the industry as a proportion of GDP, has jumped from 37.9 per cent in 1996 to 107.13 per cent by June 2013 (Australian Bureau of Statistics 2013). A notable feature of figure 6.1 is the rapid growth of the SMSF sector over the past decade, which now comprises the largest segment of the superannuation industry (by number of funds and assets). Funds under management in the SMSF sector have risen from $60.9 billion (330 000 members in 166 475 funds) in 1999/2000 to $568.3 billion (1 034 497 members in 545 334 funds) by December 2014 (Australian Taxation Office 2015). SMSFs now account for 30.14 per cent of assets in the Australian pension industry and 99.35 per cent of funds, compared with 39.70 per cent and 0.04 per cent for not-for-profit (corporate plus public sector plus industry) funds and 26.13 per cent and 0.03 per cent for retail funds.

Figure 6.1: superannuation industry in Australia 1996–2013 by total assets ($ billion)

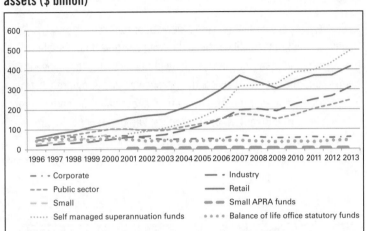

Source: Raftery (2014).

It is never too late to start putting money into super, but the earlier you can start the better because small amounts added when you are young can make a big difference to the size of your savings in retirement.

Super funds can invest in shares, property, term deposits and managed funds and they enjoy very generous tax concessions, with complying super funds receiving more favourable tax treatment than companies and individuals earning over $18 200.

Tax fact

The tax rate for a complying superannuation fund on its net income and contributions is 15 per cent. Contributions are taxed at 30 per cent if they are for individuals with income greater than $300 000. Capital gains tax is reduced to 10 per cent when assets are held for at least one year.

Part VI will focus on different ways to give your super a boost and how to access it in the most tax-effective way.

Pitfall

Before you roll over monies into a new super fund, check to see if you have an insurance policy attached to your existing fund. People with longstanding insurance cover will need to renew it if they move into an SMSF, and may fail new conditions such as declaring pre-existing conditions. Ask your old fund if there is a 'continuation option' that will allow you to buy a private policy without having to provide medical evidence.

 Tip

If you start a new job, chances are that you are earning more than your previous role. How about using some of that money to make extra contributions to superannuation via salary sacrifice? The sooner you start saving, the bigger your retirement kitty will be.

 Bonus resources

For more information on superannuation and tax go to the ATO's website www.ato.gov.au/super.

64 *Contribution limits*

The quickest way to grow your super fund balance is to make significant contributions into the fund over time and then enjoy the benefits of watching money make money.

Tip

If you are under 50 years of age and earn less than $300 000 you can contribute up to $30 000 per year into super and only pay 15 per cent tax. The contribution limit figure increases to $35 000 if you are aged 50 or over. While you don't have access today, it is your money and you can build up your net wealth quicker instead of paying up to 49 per cent in tax.

There are two kinds of contribution that can be made to a super fund:

▶ concessional contributions (before tax)

▶ non-concessional contributions (after tax).

Concessional contributions, taxed at 15 per cent (or 30 per cent if the individual earns more than $300 000), are known as before-tax contributions because the contributor, usually an employer, can claim an income tax deduction for them. They include all compulsory super guarantee contributions, salary-sacrifice contributions, and any personal contributions that you intend to claim as a tax deduction.

Tax fact

Since 1 July 2014, the concessional contributions limit is $35 000 for all individuals aged 50 and over.

 Pitfall

If you have more than one fund, all concessional contributions made to all your funds are added together and count towards the cap.

Non-concessional contributions are not taxed by the ATO and they include personal contributions you make after tax.

Tip

If you don't claim a tax deduction for any personal contributions made into super, and you earn less than $50 454, then you may be eligible for the super co-contribution.

The ATO caps the non-concessional contributions you can make each year before you pay extra tax at six times the concessional contributions cap — that is, $180 000. The untaxed plan cap of benefits that have not been subject to contributions tax within a super fund is $1 395 000 for 2015–16.

Tip

According to the ATO, if you are under 65 years old for at least one day of the financial year, you can bring forward two years' worth of contributions, giving you a total non-concessional contributions cap of $540 000 for the three years, rather than a $180 000 cap in each year of the three years. The period begins in the first year that you contribute more than the non-concessional contribution cap.

Tax fact

The date that your super fund receives your contributions can also be important as contributions are counted towards the caps in the year in which they are received and credited by your super fund. A cheque sent at the end of June but not received by the super fund until July will count towards the next financial year's cap.

Pitfall

Any amount over the concessional contributions cap will be taxed at an additional 32 per cent while any amount over the non-concessional cap attracts 47 per cent tax. You're liable for this tax, but you can use a release authority from the ATO to access your super fund monies to pay the amount. Individuals who breach the concessional contributions cap for the first time by $10 000 or less, for the 2011–12 and 2012–13 financial years only, can choose to take excess concessional contributions out of their super fund.

Excess concessional contributions are included in an individual's taxable income and taxed at their marginal tax rate (plus an interest charge) regardless of their income or the cause of the breach. The individual can choose to pay the tax bill from their own sources, or use their after-tax excess concessional contribution from super.

 Proposed change

It was announced in the 2014–15 federal budget that individuals will be provided with the option of withdrawing superannuation contributions in excess of the non-concessional contributions cap made from 1 July 2013 and any associated earnings, with these earnings to instead be taxed at the individual's marginal tax rate.

65 *Compulsory employer contributions*

When you are employed, your employer must pay super (known as superannuation guarantee (SG) contributions) on your behalf into a complying super fund. The introduction of the compulsory SG in 1992 has seen a huge boost in superannuation balances for Australians over the past two decades.

SG contributions are paid every quarter by your employer at a minimum of 9.50 per cent of your ordinary time earnings, up to the maximum contribution base. The payments count towards your concessional contributions cap. You may be able to choose the fund that this super is paid into, provided it is a complying super fund.

Tax fact

The government has strengthened the tax laws to counter fraudulent phoenix activity (where companies intentionally accumulate debts to improve cash flow or wealth and then liquidate to avoid paying the debt). The law changes are designed to protect workers' entitlements and strengthen directors' obligations by:

▶ extending the director penalty regime and the estimates regime to include the unpaid superannuation guarantee charge

▶ ensuring that directors cannot discharge their director penalties by placing their company into administration or liquidation when any pay as you go (PAYG) withholding or superannuation guarantee charge remains unpaid and unreported three months after the date that it is due for payment

▶ making directors and their associates liable to PAYG withholding non-compliance tax.

From 1 July 2021, the SG will increase by 0.5 per cent rises each financial year until the SG reaches 12 per cent in 2025–26.

You are only entitled to have SG contributions paid on your behalf from your boss if you are aged 18 years and over and you are paid $450 or more before tax in a month. It doesn't matter whether your employment status is full time or casual or if you're only a temporary resident of Australia.

Pitfall

If you're under 18 you must work more than 30 hours per week in order to be entitled to have super contributions paid on your behalf.

Contractors who are paid wholly or principally for their labour are considered employees for SG purposes and must have 9.50 per cent SG contributions paid on their behalf under the same scenario as employees.

Ordinary time earnings are used to work out any SG contributions payable for employees. They are usually what you earn during ordinary hours of work and include allowances, bonuses, commissions and any over-award payments. Ordinary time earnings exclude annual leave loadings, expense reimbursements and any overtime payments.

Tax fact

The maximum contribution base limits the maximum amount of super support that employers have to provide each quarter. It's indexed annually. For the 2015–16 year the limit is $50 810 per quarter (equivalent to an annual salary of $203 240). Your employer doesn't have to pay SG contributions for any earnings above this limit.

Tip

If you are worried that your employer isn't paying the correct amount of super into your fund, the first thing to do is to double check with them. If your query isn't resolved you can contact the ATO, which will follow up further with an investigation into your employer's affairs.

Tax fact

Employers must include the date that they intend to pay accrued superannuation on payslips provided to employees. Employers must also advise of the date that they last paid contributions on behalf of employees.

Bonus resources

Go to my website www.mrtaxman.com.au for an employee superannuation guarantee tool to determine your eligibility for the SG and to help you work out if you have received the correct amount.

66 *Salary sacrifice*

Perhaps the most tax-effective way to contribute money into super is via salary-sacrifice contributions, where you enter into an agreement with your employer to have some of your salary paid into your super fund instead of being paid to you. This has significant tax advantages if you earn over $18 200 (where the marginal tax rate jumps from zero to 20.5 per cent) as the contribution into super is only taxed at 15 per cent. Salary-sacrifice contributions count towards the concessional contributions cap.

Tip

Salary sacrificing into superannuation is one of the best legitimate ways of minimising your income tax bill.

The benefits of salary sacrificing include:

▶ super contributions are deductible for your employer

▶ your assessable income is reduced and potentially subject to a lower marginal rate

▶ money put into super is only taxed at 15 per cent instead of your marginal tax rate (potentially 49 per cent).

Example

In the 2015–16 year, Joan and Cleo both work at XYZ Ltd, earning $68 000 a year. Cleo entered into a salary-sacrifice arrangement with her employer to sacrifice $30 000 of her earnings into her super fund. Joan didn't salary sacrifice any of her salary.

Table 6.1 shows the difference between Joan and Cleo's assessable income and rates of tax at the end of the income year.

Table 6.1: example of salary-sacrifice benefits

	Joan	Cleo
Gross salary	$68 000	$68 000
Less super salary sacrifice	—	$30 000
Assessable income	$68 000	$38 000
Deductions	$1000	$1000
Taxable income	$67 000	$37 000
Income tax	$13 322	$3 572
Medicare levy (2%)	$1 340	$740
Tax on super contribution (15%)	—	$4 500
Less: low-income tax offset	—	$445
Total tax paid	**$14 662**	**$8 367**

Source: © Australian Taxation Office for the Commonwealth of Australia.

 Pitfall

If you earn under $20 542 you are better off taking your money rather than salary sacrificing extra into super as you are effectively paying no tax at this level (see p. 17). Don't pay 15 per cent contributions tax when you can pay nil.

On the downside, salary sacrificing into super can have some negatives:

▶ Any super guarantee payments are based on your reduced salary (unless you negotiate otherwise).

▶ The salary-sacrificed amount counts towards your employer's super guarantee obligations.

▶ The concessional tax rate of 15 per cent is capped at $30 000 into super each year ($35 000 for those individuals aged 50 or over). The rate increases to 30 per cent for individuals with income greater than $300 000.

▶ Any salary-sacrificed amounts will be reportable employer superannuation contributions that are included on your payment summary and will affect the income tests for the Medicare levy surcharge and some tax offsets and government benefits.

▶ Money can be tied up in super and you have to wait until retirement to access it.

▶ Payment of the sacrificed amounts above the compulsory SG is not required by regulation to be made quarterly, as is the SG.

▶ Some employers neglect to pay employees' super, particularly if they are close to bankruptcy and are having cash-flow difficulties.

 Pitfall

Salary sacrifice is a relatively straightforward strategy, but it's crucial that you crunch the numbers correctly because any contributions made that exceed the respective cap will be taxed at 47 per cent rather than the 15 per cent (or 30 per cent) concessional tax rate.

Super co-contribution

The term 'super co-contribution' should really be labelled as 'free money'! But it is surprising how few people actually take advantage of this great benefit.

Super co-contribution has been a government initiative since 2005 to help grow the superannuation balances for low and middle income earners. If you earn less than $50454, you can take advantage of the super co-contribution payment by making a maximum personal super contribution of $1000 into your super fund. The government will then match it by 50 per cent up to a further $500.

If you qualify for the co-contribution, you do not need to do anything other than make the actual personal super contributions to your super fund and lodge your income tax return. There is no separate form or application to complete. The personal super contribution must be paid into a complying super fund and must not have been claimed as an income tax deduction. You can contact your super fund to find out how to make such a contribution.

 Tip

At the start of each tax year, organise with your payroll department to have $20 taken out of your pay each week as a post-tax contribution into superannuation. You will find that this is a lot easier than trying to find $1000 in the last week in June.

The ATO outlines the two income tests you must satisfy to be eligible for the super co-contribution:

▶ the income threshold test

▶ the 10 per cent eligible income test.

The income threshold test

According to the ATO, if your total income (assessable income plus reportable fringe benefits total plus reportable employer super contributions less allowable deductions) is under the lower income threshold of $35 454 and you contribute $1000 post-tax into your super fund, the government will match it with a further $500. The super co-contribution gradually phases out to nil (by 3.333 cents per dollar) at the higher income threshold of $50 454.

The 10 per cent eligible income test

The ATO outlines that at least 10 per cent of your total income (assessable income plus reportable fringe benefits total plus reportable employer super contributions) must come from employment-related activities or carrying on a business, otherwise you will not be eligible for the co-contribution.

Example

Luke is an employee whose assessable income, reportable fringe benefits and reportable super contributions total $39 000. During the 2015–16 year he contributes $3000 as a personal super contribution to his super fund.

Luke will receive $382 from the government as a co-contribution calculated as follows:

$$\$500 - [(\$39\,000 - \$35\,454) \times \$0.03333]$$

 Pitfall

You are not entitled to a super co-contribution for any personal contributions that you have chosen to claim and that have been allowed as a tax deduction.

Tax fact

You need to provide your TFN to your super fund before it can accept any personal super contributions, including the superannuation co-contribution. There is no tax on these contributions.

If you don't see any super co-contribution payment on your annual super fund statement (or it is different from what you have calculated), contact the ATO.

FAQ

My teenage daughter works part-time after school. Can she put money into super and get the co-contribution from the government or does she need to wait until she is over 18?

There are three key conditions in order to be eligible for the co-contribution. First, you must make a post-tax (non-concessional) contribution into your super fund. Second, you must be under 71 years of age. Finally, you must pass the two income tests — the 10 per cent eligible income and threshold (under $50 454) tests. As your daughter should satisfy all of these conditions I would recommend that she puts up to $1000 into her super fund so that the government matches it with an extra $500.

68 *Transferring foreign super*

Many Australians have worked overseas and accrued retirement benefits in foreign super funds. Depending on the rules of your foreign super fund you may be able to transfer an amount from a foreign super fund to either a complying Australian super fund or yourself.

Pitfall

The transferred amounts will count towards your contributions caps, outlined earlier, and you may have to pay excess contributions tax if they exceed these caps. You or your fund may have to pay income tax on some or the entire amount. There may also be some tax obligations in the foreign country.

Prior to your Australian super fund accepting any transfer of foreign super monies, the following conditions must be met:

▶ *Age.* Contributions, other than SG contributions where there is no age limit, can be accepted if you are under 70; people who are aged between 70 and 74 must meet the 'work test'.

▶ *TFN.* You have provided your TFN to your super fund.

▶ *Contribution limit.* The transfer doesn't exceed your fund-capped contribution limit where, on 1 July of the financial year, you are:

☐ 65 or older—the limit is the non-concessional contributions cap for that income year

☐ 64 or younger—the limit is three times the non-concessional contributions cap for that income year.

Tax fact

People aged between 70 and 74 years must work a minimum of 40 hours in a 30-day period in the income year if they wish to make a contribution into super.

Example

Pierre is 71 and transfers his super interest of $248 000 from France to Australia. He satisfied the work test but his fund-capped contribution limit is only $180 000 and his Australian fund must return the excess $68 000 to his French super fund. He must wait to transfer the excess funds until the next financial year.

You also need to pay income tax on the 'applicable fund earnings' component of a foreign fund transfer. These are the earnings on your foreign super balance that have accrued only since you became an Australian resident. None of your foreign super is treated as applicable fund earnings if you transfer it to Australia within six months of becoming an Australian resident.

 Tip

According to the ATO, if you elect to include some of your applicable fund earnings in your super fund's assessable income, rather than your own, your fund will pay the tax on the amount at 15 per cent, which could be less than the marginal rate of tax that you have to pay.

Example

Ryan emigrated to Australia in September 2009 when his foreign super balance was the equivalent of A$250 000. In May 2015, he transferred the balance to his Australian super fund when it was valued at A$350 000.

If Ryan makes no election, he must declare the $100 000 of 'applicable fund earnings' in his personal assessable income for the year which is taxed at his marginal tax rates. If he elects to include the applicable fund earnings into his super fund's assessable income, it is taxed at 15 per cent within the fund.

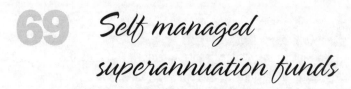

69 Self managed superannuation funds

As the name implies, a self managed super fund (SMSF) is a type of super fund that the members manage for their own benefit. SMSFs are growing in popularity as members' balances rise and they become more knowledgeable about managing their retirement savings. Over 33 000 new SMSFs were established in 2013–14 alone. The attractiveness of the concessional tax rules for super funds means that similar growth is expected to continue for some time yet.

> **Tax fact**
>
> The annual SMSF levy paid to the ATO is $259, payable in advance.

> **Tax fact**
>
> According to the ATO, there are now over 1 035 000 members within 545 000 SMSFs in Australia holding over $568 billion in retirement assets.

If you have the time as well as the expertise, including advisers that you can call on, to devote to managing your investments, setting up an SMSF may be an option for you to look at for your retirement future.

Tip

When considering the minimum balance to establish your own SMSF, you need to consider not only the amount and number of members, but also your risk profile because administration fees do vary among different investment strategies and they can eat up the benefits of doing it yourself. Results from my thesis indicate that, assuming the average expense ratio of 1.18 per cent for industry and retail funds, SMSFs are cost-effective for all balances when implementing a 100 per cent cash investment strategy, but are only cost-effective from $225 000 for sole members with a conservative profile, increasing to $325 000 for Balanced, $375 000 for Growth and $775 000 for High Growth (Raftery 2014).

Benefits of having an SMSF include:

▶ freedom to decide how and where to invest your superannuation funds

▶ tax benefits:

    ☐ the maximum tax payable on contributions is 30 per cent and only 15 per cent for earnings in a complying SMSF

    ☐ earnings in the pension phase are not taxable

▶ economies of scale — when family members (up to four) combine their superannuation funds the whole can become greater than the sum of its parts

▶ ability to invest in direct share portfolios — resulting imputation credits on dividends can help reduce the overall tax to be paid by the fund

▶ ability to invest in business real property

▶ deductible life insurance premiums

▶ rollover benefits — on retirement, assets can be rolled over into the pension phase and any capital gains subsequently realised will have no tax payable.

While SMSFs can be great, they are not ideal for everyone. Before you establish one you should think carefully about some of the following issues:

▶ *Administrative obligations.* These may be onerous and include:

☐ arranging an annual audit of your fund

☐ keeping appropriate records

☐ reporting to the ATO on the fund's operation.

▶ *Annual charges.* Fees for administration, accounting, tax and audit can be expensive and range between $2000 and $6000 for an average-sized fund.

▶ *Compliance.* You need to be aware of the requirements of being an SMSF trustee as you are responsible for ensuring the fund complies with its trust deed and superannuation laws.

▶ *Management.* You need to manage the fund's investments in the best interests of fund members including ensuring they are for the sole purpose of providing retirement benefits and keeping them separate from the personal and business affairs of fund members.

Pitfall

If a SMSF loses its complying status because it didn't follow the laws and rules, it may incur the financial penalty of being taxed at 45 per cent instead of the concessional tax rate.

FAQ

I'm thinking about setting up a SMSF. If I do, can I use my super monies to trade?

I would be extremely cautious about trading via a SMSF because super funds are technically not allowed to operate a business. I would encourage any share activities to be done as an investor rather than as a trader. You can purchase (and sell) exchange traded options as part of a hedging strategy but any premiums paid (or received) will need to be shown as CGT events. Remember that any investing must be in accordance with your written investment strategy for the fund in order to comply with the *SIS Act*. Be particularly careful with any investment in CFDs as funds deposited as security for obligations to pay margins will contravene the *SIS Act* as this is effectively a charge over fund assets.

70 *Buying property within SMSFs*

A lot of people say that they don't believe in super and prefer to own bricks and mortar as a means of funding their retirement. But a growing number of people realise they can buy property through the use of their SMSF monies.

'Property is my super' is what they say. But why not property *within* your super?

Tip

Purchase an investment property within your super fund. Don't pay for a property based on post-tax dollars, at as much as 49 per cent, when you can acquire one based on only 15 per cent! Also it is preferable to pay 10 per cent or even no tax on any capital gains rather than 24.5 per cent.

Property is becoming a very popular asset class in super funds. This is primarily due to favourable tax rates but also because, as super fund balances grow over time, the ability to acquire a property within an SMSF becomes more achievable. Superannuation is also generally protected from 'creditors and predators' and thus makes a secure vehicle for asset protection purposes.

Tax fact

According to the ATO, real property within SMSFs grew from $15.2 billion in 2003–04 to $90.9 billion in December 2014.

As identified earlier, if you own property in an SMSF, any rental income or gains generated in the SMSF will be concessionally taxed, but once you convert the SMSF into a pension these incomes and gains will become tax-free in the fund. Any tax can be reduced depending on the SMSF's investment strategy, such as excess franking credits.

Any SMSF members who receive pension income are concessionally taxed until they reach age 60, at which time this income becomes tax-free to them. With potentially no tax to pay in retirement, there is a sense of utopia while also being able to live in one of the best countries in the world.

An SMSF can purchase any type of property from unrelated parties but can only purchase commercial property, which must be wholly and exclusively used in one or more businesses, from related entities and individuals. It is important that your SMSF has a written investment strategy that allows for the holding of property.

 Tip

To increase your return on super you generally have to take on greater risk. But your investment strategy needs to match your risk profile. Some returns may be too good to be true so don't fall into the trap of chasing them. Remember that 5 per cent of something is always a lot better than 50 per cent of nothing. Do your research first. If you have sufficient funds in your super that would fund five retirements, don't take unnecessary risks. A risky strategy will only aggravate the conservative investor if the market falls. It is strongly recommended that you talk to a financial adviser. You wouldn't let an amateur build your house, so why do the same with your super?

Some issues to consider before owning real property in an SMSF are as follows.

▶ *Home ownership.* You cannot live in the property owned by your SMSF for private purposes.

▶ *Related business leases.* Commercial properties can be leased to a related business entity but only if there is a written lease in place.

▶ *Costs.* Establishment and ongoing annual costs of administration of an SMSF will rise with having a property.

▶ *Funds.* Your fund must have enough money to effect the purchase of property.

▶ *Borrowing.* You may consider whether your SMSF should borrow part of the cost to acquire the property.

▶ *Diversification.* You may consider whether your super fund has an adequate diversification of assets.

▶ *Liquidation.* You may consider the liquidation of assets required should a member retire or die.

71 Gearing through a super fund

They say that money makes money and borrowing is one of the easiest ways of building wealth, particularly within the concessionally taxed environment of superannuation.

Tax fact

Legislative changes introduced in September 2007 allow SMSFs to borrow via instalment warrants.

A gearing strategy within a super fund is not suitable for everyone as there are risks involved. With an instalment warrant, an SMSF can pay a part of an asset upfront and borrow the rest. While the debt is owing, the asset is held in trust but the SMSF maintains the beneficial interest in it. The SMSF will have the right, but not the obligation, to acquire the legal ownership of the asset through the payment of instalments.

Tip

While there has been anecdotal evidence suggesting that SMSFs borrow significant amounts of money, as at December 2014 there was only $9.4 billion borrowed by SMSFs via limited recourse borrowing arrangements. Hardly a huge amount compared to the amount of property that SMSFs invest in ($90.9 billlion).

If an SMSF acquires a portfolio of shares via an instalment warrant, the SMSF receives dividends that are generally used to pay down the loan. The SMSF may also use instalment warrants to purchase properties.

Example

Bob has $400 000 of cash sitting in his super fund. His super fund borrows a further $200 000, via an instalment warrant, in order to acquire a $600 000 property. Rental income, together with further super contributions by Bob, will go towards paying off the borrowing. Interest charged is a tax deduction for the fund.

Tip

Borrow within your super fund to purchase a share portfolio. Interest payments will be deductible within the super fund and offset tax on any dividend income. Franking credits can be used against other fund income. There is also potentially no capital gains tax depending on the eventual sale of the portfolio.

SMSFs can borrow money only if the purchase is structured correctly, but as banks become a lot more accustomed to lending to SMSFs, this type of borrowing is not as complicated as a few years ago.

There are special rules that govern borrowings within SMSFs, including the following:

▸ Any borrowing by an SMSF must only be for the acquisition of an asset.

▸ The lender is limited in recourse to the asset itself and not any other asset of the fund.

▸ Legal title to the asset must be owned by a custodian trustee explicitly for the benefit of the SMSF.

▸ Any improvements required for an investment property following its acquisition must be paid using the available resources of the SMSF and not borrowed funds.

 Pitfall

Interest rates associated with gearing within super are generally higher than normal home loan rates and need to be factored into any net return analysis.

 Proposed change

The 2014 Financial Systems Inquiry recommended that the ability for SMSFs to borrow via instalment warrants should cease. At date of publication, the Federal Government has not taken this recommendation any further.

☼ **Tip**

While super funds can gear up to 75 per cent (depending on the borrower's restrictions), you should consider falling asset values and restrict borrowing limits to no more than 50 per cent.

? **FAQ**

Can my super fund purchase an apartment 'off the plan'?

It is possible but you will need to be careful because there can be some issues along the way. The deposit, stamp duty and any other costs to secure the purchase upfront must be paid using existing cash funds in super. Only when the unit is completed and strata titled can finance be used to complete the purchase. Seeking professional advice is recommended.

---

72 *Accessing your super*

Provided your super fund's deed allows it, you can access your super:

▶ when you retire after reaching your preservation age

▶ when you turn 65

▶ under the transition to retirement rules, while continuing to work.

Your preservation age, different from your pension age, is the age you must reach before you can access your super and depends on when you were born. The preservation age, currently 55, is gradually increasing to age 60 by 1 July 2024.

Tax fact

If you leave a job after age 60, you can claim your superannuation as a lump sum or as an income stream, despite starting another job.

Tip

Temporary residents who have left Australia can apply to have their Australian super paid out to them.

Whether or not the ATO taxes your withdrawal of super funds will depend on your age and whether your super fund is a taxed or untaxed fund.

Most people have their super monies in a taxed super fund, where tax has already been paid on contributions going in and on earnings derived. If you are 60 years or older, any funds that you withdraw from your super fund will be tax-free if the fund is a taxed source. If you're under 60 the taxable component is treated as assessable income.

Regardless of your age, any income from an untaxed fund needs to be shown as assessable income in your tax return and is taxed at your marginal rate.

Tip

It is best to wait until you turn 60 to access your super as there is no tax payable on lump sum withdrawals. However, if you are under 60 (but over 55) and need to access your super, try to limit the amount you withdraw to the 'low rate cap amount', currently $185 000 (increasing to $195 000 in 2015–16), as this component is tax-free. Any amounts accessed above this amount are taxed at 17 per cent.

If you haven't reached preservation age, accessing your super before you retire is only allowed in very limited circumstances, such as you:

▶ are suffering from severe financial hardship

▶ are eligible on compassionate grounds

▶ have a terminal medical condition (certified that you are likely to die within two years)

▶ have a permanent or temporary incapacity.

You will also need to ask your super fund if you are able to withdraw super prior to reaching preservation age as the fund may have special restrictions attached as well.

 Pitfall

Early access to super may result in imprisonment even if they are your own funds!

Beware of promoters offering various plans to gain early access to your super savings before you retire. No matter what reason they provide, these schemes are illegal and heavy penalties can apply if you are not careful.

 Transition to retirement

Some people simply love their job and don't have any intention to retire. Others would love to reduce the number of hours they work but need the cash to survive. Most people think that you have to retire or resign from your job to trigger a release of your super but under the transition to retirement (TtR) rules, you can withdraw some of your super as regular payments to supplement your income.

Tax fact

If you are over 55 you can commence a transition to retirement (TtR) pension and access up to 10 per cent of your super each year tax-free to supplement your income. Once you start a pension, the fund's earnings are no longer taxed.

Once you reach your preservation age, you can access your super before you retire but only in the form of a non-commutable income stream and not as a lump sum. So once you turn 55, you can reduce your working hours without leaving your job or reducing your income. If you want, you can also top up your income with a regular income stream from your superannuation savings.

☀️ **Tip**

If you commence a TtR, salary sacrifice any surplus income (up to contribution limits) back into superannuation. This will save some tax along the way and help you to accumulate even more benefits for your retirement nest egg. Structured correctly, your day-to-day income may remain basically the same, but your superannuation retirement balance can be significantly increased.

The only specific limit on the amount of super benefits that may be withdrawn each year under the TtR rules is that it is no more than 10 per cent of the member's account balance at the start of the income year.

TtR income streams are taxed just like all other income streams. If you have reached your preservation age, but are under 60, the taxable part of your income stream will be taxed at your marginal tax rate. You will also be entitled to a 15 per cent tax offset. Once you turn 60, any income from a taxed super fund will be tax-free.

TtR arrangements can be complex to establish and manage, and it is recommended that you see an expert to help you decide if this is right for you.

> ### 💣 Pitfall
>
> A TtR pension may reduce the lifespan of your fund entitlements unless your fund has sufficient funds that generate earnings greater than your pension payments or you supplement it with extra super contributions via salary sacrifice.

> ### ❓ FAQ
>
> **If I want to take up a TtR pension do I need to reduce my work hours?**
>
> You can continue to work full-time while you are accessing up to 10 per cent of your superannuation each year. Or you may elect to gradually reduce the number of days that you work and use the TtR to supplement part of your income foregone. You could even take on more hours and perform a second job while also drawing down a TtR pension. It is up to you (and your employer) once you have reached preservation age.

74 *Account-based pensions*

Some people don't trust themselves with a lump sum and prefer to be disciplined by receiving regular payments. There is no requirement to withdraw all of your super just because you turn a certain age. Instead you may elect to convert your superannuation fund from the accumulation phase into the pension phase and start an income stream, such as an account-based pension (previously known as an allocated pension).

Income streams receive favourable tax treatment, another reason why people elect to start an account-based pension. Individuals who cash out their super may have to pay income tax on any earnings but these earnings would be tax-free in a pension environment.

Tax fact

In the accumulation stage, superannuation funds pay tax at 15 per cent (or 30 per cent on contributions if the individual earns more than $300 000) but once an account-based pension is started, the fund pays no tax at all on its earnings.

The tax-free environment of pension funds provides special opportunities to avoid CGT on assets held within super funds that have accumulated large unrealised capital gains.

Tip

Based on the current tax laws, consider converting your super fund into an account-based pension fund and pay no tax on the subsequent disposal of share portfolios or investment properties held within the fund.

The ATO has outlined that if you reach your preservation age, but are under age 60, the taxable component of your income stream will be taxed at your marginal tax rate and if it is paid from a taxed source, you also receive a 15 per cent tax offset. For those 60 and over, your income from a taxed source will be tax-free.

Pitfall

According to the ATO, once you start a pension or annuity, a minimum amount, based on your age, is required to be paid to you each year. There is no maximum amount other than the balance of your super account.

Table 6.2 shows the minimum percentage factor for each age group.

Table 6.2: minimum percentage age factors

Age	Minimum % withdrawal
Under 65	4
65–74	5
75–79	6
80–84	7
85–89	9
90–94	11
95 or more	14

Source: © Australian Taxation Office for the Commonwealth of Australia.

75 *Death benefits*

Since superannuation became compulsory over 20 years ago, retirement nest eggs have grown substantially and are an integral part of most estate planning. Premature death may mean a large payment to family members, particularly when a life insurance policy is attached to the fund.

Tip

Superannuation does not form part of your estate. If you don't put a 'binding nomination' in place, the trustee of your super fund has absolute discretion in distributing your super benefits to anyone he or she pleases.

To ensure that your super funds are properly dealt with upon your death, make a 'binding nomination' with the super fund trustee. Binding nominations must be witnessed by two independent individuals and expire every three years, so make sure that you always update them.

Tax fact

Unlike other countries, there is no inheritance tax in Australia. But don't be fooled because there are three things in life that are certain: taxes, death ... and taxes on death!

If a death benefit is going to a dependant, such as a spouse or minor children, then it can be paid either as an income stream or as a lump-sum amount. Lump-sum payments to dependants are tax-free. However, a death benefit can only be paid as a lump sum to a non-dependant.

The popularity of superannuation as a low-tax environment within which to grow wealth, coupled with longer life expectancies, has resulted in an increasing number of financially independent people receiving a superannuation death benefit from a parent.

Pitfall

Lump-sum payments to non-dependants are taxed at 17 per cent on the taxed element while the untaxed element is taxed at a maximum rate of 32 per cent.

If you don't have a dependant to pay your death benefit to, there are a few strategies that you can use that can make a big difference to the final amount of tax payable. Accordingly, it is recommended that you discuss succession issues with a professional adviser.

If you are suffering from a terminal illness, you may want to consider withdrawing your entire super as a lump sum tax-free so that upon death it passes through your will to your independent family members tax-free as well.

Alternatively, consider withdrawing your super and then making non-concessional super contributions up to the $180 000 limit each year so that any superannuation death benefit will comprise a tax-free element.

 Tip

A child-allocated pension is a smart way for a child to inherit their parent's super together with any linked life insurance. To make sure that a child pension can be activated when it's needed, the super fund needs to have the child listed as a beneficiary of their parent's account.

---

76 *Lost or unclaimed super*

We work hard for our money, so it is surprising that so many people ignore one of their biggest assets: super. You should always keep track of your super by checking your annual statements for employer contributions, fees and insurance cover, and you should analyse fund performance in general.

Tip

You may have worked in 12 different jobs but that is no excuse to have a dozen super funds. They are too hard to manage and may be eaten up in fees. Consolidate them by rolling them all into one fund. Make sure you arrange adequate replacement life insurance if you had coverage in existing accounts before closing them down.

Tax fact

According to the ATO, there is currently over $12.5 billion in lost super in Australia. Since 2014, the ATO has started consolidating accounts with low balances (initially under $1000 but increasing to $10 000) by providing details of these accounts to members' current funds.

Starting a new job can be exciting but also nerve-racking at the same time. The turnover in the Australian workforce is greater than ever, with the Australian Bureau of Statistics estimating that about 1.8 million people change jobs every year. If you do change your job, do not neglect your super. It can be very easy to forget it, particularly if you change both job and address, as you may not get statements in the future. It is wise to arrange for your super from past jobs to be rolled over into your new account.

Tip

You may have some lost super if you have changed your name (for example, through marriage), your address or your job. Ensure that you notify all of your super funds when you change address or you may risk losing touch with your funds.

SuperSeeker (www.ato.gov.au/superseeker) is a free online super search tool provided by the ATO to help you search for any lost and unclaimed super. Your search can be completed in a couple of minutes as you only need to supply your name, date of birth and TFN.

 Tip

Simply fill in an electronic form on the ATO's SuperSeeker webpage www.ato.gov.au/superseeker and arrange to consolidate lost superannuation accounts online.

If SuperSeeker finds a match it will provide a list of all accounts on the lost members register (LMR) as well as any other unclaimed super amounts held by the ATO. Any lost super listed on the LMR is held by the relevant super funds.

Where an account is found on the LMR, you should:

▶ contact the super fund to update them with your personal details

▶ consolidate your super funds

▶ withdraw your benefit, if your account balance is less than $200 and certain criteria are met.

Tax fact

Superannuation funds that hold more than one account for the same individual are required to consolidate those accounts where possible so that members do not have to pay unnecessary fees and other charges on multiple accounts.

Tip

If you have more than one super account, consider rolling them all into one super fund and save on fees as well as being able to manage your super more easily. Many funds make it easier for you by providing a 'consolidation' service, but make sure you check what your fund will charge you before you close the account and whether you'll lose any benefits.

Tax fact

Since 1 January 2013, lost or inactive superannuation accounts with balances under $2000 are transferred to the ATO, increasing to $2500 in 2016 and $3000 in 2017. Since 1 July 2013, the ATO has been paying interest on all lost super accounts reclaimed.

Tip

The best advice that I can give about superannuation is to start at a young age, but sadly most people don't think about their retirement income until it is almost too late in life. The thought of superannuation may be dull and boring when you are 21, but it really is one of the best investment vehicles for your money. Money makes money so the quicker you can build up your nest egg, the less risk that you will need to take later in life. There are tax savings for salary sacrificing into super with as much as 34 per cent for those in the highest tax bracket. Most people will save at least $1650 in tax for every $10 000 sacrificed. That adds up over time.

Part VII

Your business

There comes a time in everyone's life when you think — even for just one moment — about running your own business. As a business owner myself I can tell you that running a business is gratifying and can offer you many rewards and benefits. But it brings with it quite a few nightmares along the way.

Before you get too caught up in complicated tax structures and tax planning, the first thing you must consider is whether you are actually running a business or merely practising a hobby. The nature of your trading activity will largely determine if you are running a business or not. The ATO generally looks at trading volume as the key indicator for determining any tax implications.

> **Tax fact**
>
> According to the ATO, over 50 000 Australians now derive a substantial source of income online.

The past few years have seen an increase in the number of people who are selling online on a full-time basis. If you are selling a few old bits and pieces from around the house that you no longer use, the ATO sees this activity as merely a 'hobby' and the income is not assessable. But if you start selling new items as well as actively trading second-hand 'bargains' that you pick up along the way, the ATO views you as 'being in business' and any profits that you derive as being assessable.

Tip

If you are considering buying an existing business then ensure that you conduct a thorough due diligence so that you are buying the business assets but not any surprises. The purchase of a business is full of untold opportunities but also unknown problems with potential skeletons hiding in the closet.

Part VII is designed to help you stay in control of your tax affairs during the various stages of your business. Tax is the biggest expense that a business will encounter. As your business grows and changes, so will your tax situation. There will be additional tax obligations such as how to pay employees and other businesses and how to report and pay tax and superannuation.

Tax fact

When starting a business, the most common tax registrations needed include the following:

▶   a TFN (not required for sole traders as you use your existing TFN)

▶   an Australian business number (ABN)

▶   goods and services tax (GST)

▶   PAYG witholding.

Tip

When you start a new business, take advantage of the multitude of free services supported by different government departments to assist businesses in areas such as planning, marketing, budgeting, cash flow and networking. There are also a number of different grants available. See www.business.gov.au for more information.

Bonus resources

For more information on running a small business, the ATO has an excellent publication called *Tax basics for small business* (NAT 1908).

77 *Choosing the right business structure*

If you are planning to make a fortune, perhaps you should consider your business structure before you give away half of it in taxes.

Tip

According to the ATO, the particular structure chosen needs to be appropriate to the business owner's specific circumstances and take into account likely events in the future (such as getting married, having children or admitting new partners).

The structure of a business will affect:

► how much tax your business has to pay

► how other businesses deal with you

► your administration costs

► your level of asset protection.

 Tip

Small businesses need all the help they can get but simply can't afford it on a full-time basis. Don't view external advice purely as a cost exercise. Sometimes you need to pay a bit extra to surround yourself with a group of quality advisers such as an accountant and a solicitor to help get the business on the right track for financial success.

The most common structures used by Australian businesses are:

► sole traders

► partnerships

► companies

► trusts.

Sole traders

Sole traders are taxed in exactly the same way as individuals. A business enjoying good profits can expect to pay tax at the higher marginal rates. There is no asset protection if you are a sole trader so beware of 'creditors and predators'.

 Proposed change

It was announced in the 2015 federal budget that from 1 July 2015, a small business tax discount of 5 per cent of the income tax payable

Proposed change *(cont'd)*

on the business income received is available to individuals who run a business as a sole trader or partnership, capped at $1000 per individual per annum.

Partnerships

Partnerships are often preferred by husband-and-wife businesses and also where personal services are provided. They have a simple and cost-effective structure, but their major disadvantage is that they offer no asset protection. Partnerships do not pay tax in their own right. Instead, each partner pays tax on their share of the net partnership income at their marginal tax rate.

 Pitfall

Partners are each personally and separately liable for the debts of the partnership should the business fail.

Companies

A private company (with 'Pty Ltd' at the end of the business name) is the most common business structure for operating entities, particularly where capital gains are not likely and where the small business capital gains tax concessions will not apply. Unlike sole traders and partnerships, companies have limited liability, although personal guarantees may be required by directors from time to time. The corporate tax rate is a flat 30 per cent. The rate is proposed to decrease to 28.5 per cent for small companies from 1 July 2015. Careful tax planning is required for companies near the $2 million threshold level as an error could cost $6000 extra tax for those working on a 20 per cent net profit margin.

Pitfall

Loans (or debts forgiven) by private companies to their shareholders are generally treated by the ATO as unfranked dividends assessable in the individual shareholder's income tax return.

Trusts

Using a family trust is an excellent way to minimise the overall income tax liability for a business. A trust can also help with managing assets and liabilities, as well as offering flexibility for estate-planning purposes.

Tax fact

The total net income reported to the ATO by trusts in the 2012–13 financial year was $143.8 billion. This was a 2.56 per cent increase from the 2011–12 financial year.

Family trusts are not directly taxed. Instead it is the beneficiaries of the trust who are subject to income tax on their share of the trust's net income. Beneficiaries also have the ability to obtain the full benefit of any small business capital gains tax concessions and franking credits.

A company is often used to act as a corporate trustee of a trust so that the personal assets of the business owners have some form of protection from any future claims made against the entity.

Where partners are likely to be admitted, the business could be run through a unit trust with the respective units being held by a family trust.

Tip

If a business, via a family trust, is deriving substantial income and all of the individuals are on marginal tax rates in excess of the corporate tax rate, consider establishing a corporate beneficiary to limit the overall tax payable.

 Pitfall

Trustees of a discretionary trust will be assessed on 47 per cent of the trust income if they do not document their resolution for distribution of income before 30 June each year. The trust's accounts do not need to be prepared at this time.

 Proposed change

While restructuring costs (income tax, stamp duty and legal fees) can be expensive if you don't pick the right structure upfront, the government has proposed that professional expenses incurred after 1 July 2015 in relation to the establishment of a new business will be deductible in full. CGT rollover relief will also be available for small businesses to change legal structure without attracting CGT.

78 *Tax obligations*

Most business owners will tell you that they hate it, but one of the most important tasks in running a business is meeting your tax obligations. These include collecting and reporting GST, lodging business activity statements (BAS) and submitting an annual tax return.

GST

If your business has a gross business income (GST turnover) of $75 000 or more ($150 000 or more if it is a nonprofit organisation) or provides taxi travel, you will need to:

- register for GST
- charge 10 per cent GST on the price of a taxable supply
- issue tax invoices (for amounts greater than $75) to customers, showing your ABN
- report and remit GST charged on the taxable supplies to the ATO in the required instalments:
  - ☐ monthly (if turnover is *greater* than $20 million)
  - ☐ quarterly (if turnover is *less* than $20 million).

Small businesses (where turnover is less than $2 million) use the cash method of reporting, while all other businesses must use the accrual method.

GST is calculated from the GST-inclusive price as follows:

$$GST = GST\text{-inclusive price} \div 11$$

 Tip

Be disciplined and keep at least one-third of the income you receive aside to cover your GST and income tax obligations.

 Pitfall

If your business does not quote its ABN, then your payer may deduct 47 per cent withholding tax from payment.

Activity statements

Businesses are required to complete an activity statement to report and pay a number of tax obligations, such as GST, PAYG instalments, PAYG withholding and fringe benefits tax (FBT).

Tax fact

According to the ATO, the average time taken by a business to complete its business activity statement (BAS) is two hours. The average time taken to complete a company income tax return in 2012–13 was 7.1 hours.

All businesses registered for GST need to regularly lodge a BAS with the ATO on either a monthly (21 days after period end), quarterly (28 October, 28 February, 28 April and 28 July) or annual basis (before lodgement due date for income tax return). Any GST paid on purchases is offset against the GST collected from customers. The net amount is remitted to the ATO via your BAS.

Pitfall

Common GST mistakes include:
- ▶ claiming GST credits on bank fees and government charges where no GST has been charged in the first place
- ▶ not remitting GST on government grants and incentives that were received inclusive of GST
- ▶ incorrectly claiming GST credits on GST-free purchases such as basic food items, exports and some health services
- ▶ claiming the entire GST credit on a car purchased for more than the luxury car limit of $57 466 GST-inclusive
- ▶ not apportioning private usage for expenses that have GST charged.

Phased in over four years, large entities are required to make PAYG income tax instalments monthly, rather than quarterly. This will occur from:

▶ 1 January 2015 for companies with a turnover of $100 million or more

▶ 1 January 2016 for companies with a turnover of $20 million or more and all other entities in the PAYG instalment system with a turnover of $1 billion or more

▶ 1 January 2017 for all other entities in the PAYG instalment system with a turnover of $20 million or more.

FAQ

I'm about to get a car under my company and will be using it approximately 70 per cent for work and 30 per cent personal. In order to avoid FBT I will pay for my personal expenses incurred. Do I still need to register for FBT?

Yes you will still need to register for FBT and submit an FBT return each year, even if the net FBT payable is zero because you make a personal contribution.

☼ Tip

If you want to manage your business tax affairs online with the ATO, there is a Business Portal available on the ATO website. It is safe to use as your information is protected by online security credentials. You must get a digital certificate from the ATO in order to use it on your computer. You can view your statement of account, update contact details, and prepare and lodge activity statements.

> **! Tax fact**
>
> In 2013–14, the ATO conducted over 19 850 reviews and audits of employer obligations, raising over $812 million in liabilities. Over the next three years the ATO will spend $26.5 million on GST compliance activities alone.

79 *Record keeping*

While it is a legal requirement that you keep business records for tax purposes, it is also a good idea to keep excellent records in order to maximise your income tax return claims.

> **💣 Pitfall**
>
> If you do not keep proper records, the ATO can impose a penalty of up to $2200.

Excellent record-keeping practices include:

▶ maintaining a cashbook (either manually or electronically) to record all information from your bank account

▶ keeping adequate employment records, including:

    ☐ PAYG payment summaries

    ☐ employment termination payments

    ☐ reportable fringe benefits.

▶ keeping all documents in a safe and secure place for a period of five years

▶ fulfilling tax obligations such as:

   ☐ withholding PAYG tax

   ☐ recording all GST obligations

   ☐ paying superannuation contributions to complying superannuation funds.

The following is a quick checklist of the ATO requirements relating to record keeping.

Records relating to payments to employees:

▶ employee payment records

▶ employee termination payment summaries

▶ fringe benefits provided to employees

▶ PAYG payment summaries

▶ superannuation records

▶ TFN declarations

▶ withholding variation notices.

> **Tax fact**
>
> According to research conducted by Galaxy Research, 21 per cent of businesses in Australia still use a manual accounting system.

Records relating to income tax and GST:

▶ sales records:

   ☐ bank statements

   ☐ cash register tapes

   ☐ credit card statements

   ☐ deposit books

   ☐ tax invoices.

▶ purchase and expense records:

☐ bank statements

☐ chequebook butts

☐ credit card statements

☐ logbooks showing any private use

☐ tax invoices.

▶ year-end income tax records:

☐ capital gains tax records

☐ depreciation schedules

☐ list of debtors

☐ list of creditors

☐ stocktake records.

Bonus resources

For more information, the ATO has an excellent publication on *Record keeping for small business* (NAT 3029).

PAYG withholding records relating to business payments:

▶ amounts withheld from payments where no ABN was quoted

▶ PAYG withholding voluntary agreements.

☼ Tip

Computerised systems help you maintain good records of your transactions and tax invoices, manage your cash flow and make sound business decisions. They also make it easier to meet your tax obligations, and potentially save you time and money down the track.

80 *Deferring tax*

We all have to pay our fair share of taxes but if you can legitimately delay the inevitable to another tax year then you should do so. Any deferral of taxes will help cash flow as you potentially get a further 12 months before you need to pay the tax man. Tax rates may also be lower in subsequent years.

Delaying the derivation of income and bringing forward deductions are the two main ways of deferring your taxable income to the next financial year.

Deferring income

In order to work out the best way to defer assessable income to future years, you need to know how the ATO will assess your business income in the first place.

Tax fact

Your business must account for its income on either a cash basis or an accruals basis, depending on the nature of the income. You cannot freely choose which method to use. It can be a grey area but you must use the method which gives the 'substantially correct reflection' of your business.

Most small businesses will be assessed on a cash basis where income is recognised only when cash is received. Constructive receipt is important here so it is possible to minimise income by deferring receipts until after 1 July.

 Pitfall

The moment a cheque is handed over is the moment that a payment has been received on a cash basis. Not banking it will not work!

Larger businesses will need to use the accruals basis where income is recognised as it is earned and not as money is received. If your business operates on an accruals basis you may want to defer your invoicing until next tax year.

Maximise deductions

If you have annual expenses such as subscriptions and insurance due in July, pay them before 30 June to reduce this year's tax. As a small business, you can use the prepayments concession where you can claim a deduction for the total expense you prepaid if you receive the goods or services in full within 12 months. Other deductible expenses to scrutinise include bad debts, depreciation on business assets, revaluing your trading stock and making superannuation contributions before year end.

You do not need to actually have paid out any money to have 'incurred' a loss or outgoing. If you are definitively committed, or have completely subjected yourself to the expenditure, it will be deductible. Mere provisions, such as for annual leave and long-service leave, are not deductible because the employer is not definitively committed to the expenditure.

Tip

If you pay annual staff bonuses after year end, pass a resolution before 30 June and have it in writing that you are committed to the expenditure in order for it to be tax-deductible this year.

 Pitfall

If you do not pay your employees' compulsory superannuation before 30 June you are not entitled to a tax deduction for it this year, even though you are committed to the expenditure.

 Tip

If you are acquiring an existing business, consider taking out Successor Liability Insurance to limit your exposure to unknown liabilities.

81 *Trading stock*

The ATO defines trading stock as anything you produce, manufacture, acquire or purchase for manufacture, sale or exchange in your business, including livestock.

If the value of your trading stock at the end of the income year is:

▶ more than at the start of the financial year — the difference is added to your assessable income

▶ less than at the start of the financial year — a deduction can be claimed for the difference.

Small businesses only need to make an adjustment to their taxable income if their closing stock varies by more than $5000 from their opening stock figure.

Tax fact

If the value of the trading stock of a small business varies by less than $5000, you can elect to treat the value of closing stock as the same as opening stock at the start of the year for tax purposes.

An annual stocktake is usually conducted by businesses, generally as close as possible to the end of the financial year, to determine the value of trading stock on hand at 30 June.

Pitfall

If you run a business that sells food and you take an item for private use, such as milk or a meal, you must account for it as if you had sold it and include the value of the item in your taxable income. Owners can either keep a tab of the actual value of items used for private purposes or apply a standard amount from the ATO for your industry.

Tax fact

Taxation Determination TD 2015/9 provides the amount that the ATO will accept as estimates for the value of goods taken from trading stock for private use by taxpayers in different industries. Amounts range from $780 per adult per annum for a fruiterer business to $4490 per adult per annum for a licensed restaurant/cafe.

Irrespective of how they are valued for accounting purposes, there are only three methods allowed for valuing your trading stock for tax purposes:

▶ cost

▶ market selling value

▶ replacement value.

 Tip

The best stock valuation method to adopt is the method that produces the lowest value of trading stock. If you have different classes of stock then you can use a different basis of valuation for each class as well as for each individual item of stock, although these calculations can get messy.

You can change the method used each year so long as the opening stock figure is the same as the closing stock figure from the previous year.

 Tip

If you have some old plant or stock that your business simply can't sell, consider physically writing it off before 30 June and get a tax deduction for it this year.

 Bad debts

One of the things you invariably have to deal with when you are in business is customers who won't pay for your goods or services. Some customers don't have the cash flow to pay, while some will dispute the debt. And then there are those who are simply bad eggs and have no intention whatsoever of paying you.

Most businesses are required to record their income on an accruals basis for tax purposes. This means that they are required to show all sales as taxable income even if they don't receive the cash!

Some debts owed to a business can be quite sizeable, so having to pay tax on income not received can have a significant impact on cash flow. Luckily, the ATO allows a deduction for bad debts, but certain criteria must be satisfied.

Like obsolete stock, the ATO will only grant an income tax deduction for your business for a bad debt if:

▶ there was a debt in existence

▶ the debt was physically written off prior to 30 June

▶ the debt was genuinely bad by the terms of agreement or other reasonable criteria

▶ the debt was originally shown as income in the current or a previous financial year.

Pitfall

If businesses do not physically write off a debt before 30 June they are not entitled to a tax deduction in that financial year.

As the criteria require action by the business, namely writing off the debt, a review of all debts by a company before 30 June each year is crucial.

Tip

To physically write off a debt as bad, the business must do so in writing. This may take the form of a journal entry or minutes of a board meeting authorising the writing off. A mere mental note, not evidenced in writing, to treat the debt as bad will not suffice—there must be some physical evidence of writing off.

Most business owners get confused with deductions for bad debts and why there should be a nil impact for tax purposes when they have outlaid money for the goods and services in the first place. What they don't take into account is that they are already getting deductions for their costs (such as rent, wages and materials) incurred in the production of the goods.

Unfortunately, having to write off bad debts is simply a cost of running your own business. But make sure that you do so in a timely manner.

Tax fact

If your business makes a claim for a bad debt but the debtor later pays the debt, you are required to record the actual amount received in the year of receipt as assessable income.

83 Home-based businesses

Starting up a home-based business can be one of the most rewarding things that you can do. Most businesses, mine included, originally started from home. There are many benefits to working from home, including flexibility, saving on travel time and getting some extra tax deductions. There is also a bonus in not paying any extra rent.

You may be able to claim the business-related portion of the following 'running' costs:

▶ depreciation of home-office furniture, fittings and equipment such as computers and desks (certain items under $20 000 can be claimed in full by small businesses that choose the simpler depreciation rules — see tip 85 for more information).

▶ heating, cooling and lighting

▶ home telephone

▶ internet access

▶ printer and printer cartridges

▶ repairs to your home-office furniture and fittings

▶ stationery.

> ### 💣 Pitfall
>
> If you run your business from your own home, there is a possibility that your home could be subject to capital gains tax. Make sure you consult a tax adviser about your own particular circumstances. Sometimes it may be cheaper to pay for separate office space rather than incur a big tax bill in the future.

The ATO is quite particular with the claiming of home-office 'occupancy' expenses. If you genuinely operate a business from your home you are allowed to claim a proportion of mortgage interest or rent based on the actual floor space that you use for the business.

> **Tax fact**
>
> If your home is your place of business, you can also claim a deduction for your occupancy expenses including:
>
> ▶ council rates
> ▶ home-insurance premiums
> ▶ mortgage interest
> ▶ rent.

The ATO looks at a number of factors to determine if your home is your place of business. The area must be:

▶ clearly identifiable as a place of business

▶ not readily suitable for use for private purposes

▶ used almost exclusively for business purposes

▶ used regularly for visits by clients or customers.

Home office deductions are usually calculated as follows:

Floor area used × relevant expenditure ÷ total floor area

> **Example**
>
> If your home office is 6 m × 3 m (that is, 18 square metres) and the total house is 100 square metres in size, you can claim 18 per cent of your occupancy costs for income tax purposes.

Tip

If the ATO conducts an audit into your business affairs, it will not accept estimates, so you must be quite accurate with your calculations. I recommend getting your measuring tape out and writing down the dimensions of your office and your overall house. I find it also helps to strengthen your case if you take photos of your office, especially if you move house down the track.

84 *Employing people*

So you took the first step and started your own business. Now business has gone crazy and sales are through the roof and you need to hire someone else to help you in handling the growth.

While it is always exciting when a small business starts to grow and you need to employ staff for the first time, you need to be aware of some of the obligations that come with being an employer. Non-compliance could lead to penalties, which include fines and prosecution.

Wages and conditions

All issues concerning wages and employment conditions in the private sector fall under the *Fair Work Act 2009*, which requires you to maintain a minimum standard of pay, conditions and entitlements for your employees. There are 10 National Employment Standards that apply to all employers and employees.

Employment records

You must issue pay slips to each employee and keep accurate and complete time and wages records for a minimum of seven years.

Taxation obligations

Your taxation obligations include:

▶ registering with the ATO as a new employer

▶ obtaining TFN declarations (NAT 3092) from employees

▶ withholding PAYG tax from payments you make to your employees and paying it to the ATO

▶ preparing year-end PAYG payment summaries for employees

▶ calculating any employment termination payments

▶ paying fringe benefits tax for benefits paid to employees

▶ paying payroll tax if total wages exceed the exemption threshold applicable in your state or territory.

 Tip

While they need to be provided by 14 July, your employees will appreciate it if you give them their annual PAYG payment summary as soon as possible after year end so they can complete their own tax returns.

Superannuation obligations

Employing people, whether full time, part time or casual, will trigger the superannuation guarantee legislation which requires you to pay a minimum of 9.50 per cent of the earnings base (generally ordinary time earnings) into employees' choice of super fund within 28 days after the end of the quarter.

 Pitfall

If you don't pay your super obligations in time, then you are charged an interest shortfall penalty of 10 per cent per annum plus an administration fee of $20 per employee per quarter.

Holiday and leave entitlements

You need to pay public holidays for all employees except for those who are only paid for hours worked such as contract workers and casual employees. Other paid leave should include annual, sick and long-service leave.

Other employment issues to consider include

▶ anti-discrimination

▶ equal employment opportunity

▶ occupational health and safety legislation

▶ public liability insurance

▶ workers compensation.

Tip

How do good, profitable businesses go bad? Mainly because their owners took all of the cash out of their business before realising that they had to pay the tax man for GST and PAYG withholding in the quarterly BAS or income tax at the end of the year. Super payable to employees is another forgotten liability. To avoid falling into the trap, open up a separate bank account and filter one-third of your income away to cover these outgoings.

Bonus resources

Go to my website www.mrtaxman.com.au for some superannuation guarantee calculators to work out your SG contributions for your eligible employees or the SG charge if you are late in paying them.

85 *Tax concessions and offsets*

Small businesses have access to a range of concessions to help reduce their taxable income, designed to make tax administration easier. For example, they are entitled to immediate tax deductions for business expenses prepaid for 12 months in advance, such as interest.

Simplified depreciation rules

Businesses with an annual turnover under $2 million can immediately write off many depreciating assets that cost less than $20 000 exclusive of GST. For businesses that are registered for GST, the effective ticket-price threshold is $21 999 as you can claim the 10 per cent GST rebate in your quarterly business activity statement.

 Pitfall

Vehicles purchased through a company or trust structure may be subject to fringe benefits tax.

Small businesses can consolidate other assets in a general small business pool at a rate of 30 per cent. This pool can be immediately deducted if the balance is less than $20 000 before 30 June 2017.

 Tax fact

If you are 'substantially self-employed' you can claim super contributions as a personal tax deduction, as long as no more than 10 per cent of your assessable income is from salary and wages.

Proposed change

The government has proposed a change to the instant write-off threshold, with only assets costing less than $20 000 being eligible for immediate write-off for assets purchased prior to 30 June 2017. After this date the threshold will revert back to $1000 (the threshold for assets that were purchased prior to 12 May 2015).

Restart wage subsidy

Employers can receive up to $10 000 (GST inclusive) in government assistance if they hire a full-time job seeker aged 50 or older under the Restart wage subsidy program. Eligible employers will receive $3000 if the job seeker was previously unemployed for a period of 6 months and subsequently employed for at least 6 months (for a minimum of 30 hours per week). Employers will also receive further payments at 12 months ($3000), 18 months ($2000) and two years ($2000). It was proposed in the 2015–16 federal budget to reduce the timeframe for the payments to just one year. Eligible job seekers employed for between 15 and 29 hours per week will attract a pro-rata Restart wage subsidy.

Research and development tax incentive

If your business is involved in research and development (R&D) in Australia to create new or improved materials, devices, processes, products or services it may be eligible for an R&D tax incentive. The Department of Innovation, Industry, Science and Research defines R&D activity as systematic, investigative and experimental activity that:

▶ involves both innovation and high levels of technical risk

▶ is for the process of producing new knowledge
   or improvements.

The R&D tax incentive is a 45 per cent refundable tax offset (proposed to reduce to 43.5 per cent from 1 July 2014) for companies with an annual turnover less than $20 million. Since 1 July 2013, large businesses with annual Australian turnover of $20 billion or more are no longer eligible for the R&D tax incentive, but will be eligible to claim their R&D expenditure as a general deduction.

The ATO looks after this incentive jointly with AusIndustry. In order to be eligible you need to register each income year with the Industry Research and Development Board and meet the minimum R&D threshold expenditure of $20 000.

86 Selling or closing down

If you close down or sell your business, there are significant opportunities to do some tax planning and minimise CGT as much as possible.

If you are a retiring small business owner you may be entitled to disregard some or all of your capital gains if you:

▶ are 55 years or over and retired

▶ are permanently incapacitated

▶ owned your 'small business CGT assets' for 15 years or more.

If you do not satisfy the above criteria, the ATO says you may still be entitled to the following concessions to reduce any potential taxable capital gain from the sale of your small business:

▶ 50 per cent general CGT discount — for reducing capital gains on capital assets that you have held for 12 months or more

▶ small business 50 per cent active asset reduction — reduces the capital gains on 'active assets' by 50 per cent

▶ small business retirement exemption — disregards any remaining capital gain by up to a lifetime limit of $500 000 per individual if paid into a complying superannuation fund

▶ small business asset rollover — defers a capital gain where you acquire 'replacement assets'.

To qualify for these small business concessions, the ATO says you must satisfy the following conditions:

▶ You have been carrying on a business with a turnover under $2 million.

▶ The net value of your CGT assets and any related entities is a maximum of $6 million.

▶ Your CGT asset is an 'active asset'.

▶ If the asset is a share or interest in a trust:

☐ there must be a 'controlling individual' just before the CGT event

☐ the entity claiming the concession must be a 'CGT concession stakeholder' in the company.

💣 Pitfall

If you use your home as a business office it is incorrect to think that if you don't claim 'occupancy' expenses (such as a portion of the mortgage interest, insurance and council rates) you are not liable to CGT.

The law clearly states that CGT is payable on the portion of the home used for running the business when:

▶ the home was acquired after 19 September 1985
▶ part of it was used to produce income at some time when it was owned
▶ the taxpayer would be entitled to deduct interest had it been incurred on money borrowed to buy the home.

When doing capital gains tax calculations on your home used for a business, the ATO allows you to have acquired it for its market value on the day when the property was first used to produce assessable income.

☼ Tip

If you run your business from home, obtain a market valuation of your home at the time the home starts to produce income.

Bonus resources

For more information on how business sales are treated for CGT purposes, the ATO has an excellent *Guide to capital gains tax concessions for small business* (NAT 8384).

 ## Personal services income

If you are a contractor or a consultant and you operate your business via a partnership, company or trust, you need to ensure that you satisfy the personal services income (PSI) rules, as you run the risk of being personally liable for tax on the income regardless of your business structure. The rules can also deny deductions for some business-related expenses incurred as a contractor.

If the majority of your income is for labour rather than for materials supplied or tools and equipment used to complete the job, then you will be subject to the PSI rules.

There is an exemption from the PSI rules if you pass the results test, which is a test to work out if you've received the income after achieving a specific result or outcome.

To pass the results test, you need to satisfy all three of the following conditions for at least three quarters of the year:

▶ you are paid income to achieve a specified result or outcome

▶ you provide tools and equipment as contracted in order to perform the work

▶ you are liable for rectifying any defects in the work.

If you fail the results test, you need to apply an additional rule, known as the 80/20 rule, under which you can't generate more than 80 per cent of your income from one client and you must also satisfy one of the following conditions:

▶ you have received income from two or more clients who are not connected or related (unrelated clients test)

▶ you employed or contracted others to help complete the work (employment test)

▶ you used a separate premises exclusively for business (business premises test).

You can also apply for a determination from the ATO for an exemption from the rules, but it is generally only allowed in exceptional circumstances.

 Pitfall

If you fail the results and 80/20 tests for the PSI rules then you must:

▶ pay any retained profits from PSI as a salary and wage to the individual who performed the services

▶ comply with the additional PAYG obligations

▶ complete and attach a PSI schedule with your tax return

▶ not claim deductions against PSI where there is no entitlement, such as council rates, interest or rent for your home office, or payments to your spouse for secretarial work.

88 *Non-commercial losses*

Losses are sometimes unavoidable in business, particularly in the start-up years. For individuals and partnerships, if you have a net loss from a business activity, the non-commercial loss rules apply. These rules determine whether you can use your business loss to offset income from other sources, such as salary and wages, interest and dividends.

Tax fact

The non-commercial legislation was introduced to stop 'Pitt Street farmers' (the main street in the Sydney business district) from claiming huge losses on their farms, primarily used as holiday homes, against their normal salary and wage income.

Each year that a business makes a net loss, the owner must consider whether he or she can claim the loss in the current tax return or whether it's necessary to defer the loss until future profits are made.

Tax fact

The ATO will only allow you to offset your business loss against assessable income from other sources if:

▶ you run a primary production or professional arts business and certain exceptions apply

▶ you earn less than $250 000 and satisfy one of the four non-commercial losses tests (profits test, assessable income test, other assets test, real property test)

▶ the Commissioner of Taxation uses his or her discretion to allow you to claim the loss (this rarely happens).

The non-commercial losses rules limit the ability of taxpayers to offset business losses against other assessment income unless one or more of the following tests are met:

▶ assessable income generated by the business is at least $20 000 (assessable income test)

▶ the business shows a profit for at least three out of the past five years (profits test)

▶ the business has property or an interest in real property with a value of at least $500 000 on a continuing basis (real property test)

▶ the business has at least $100 000 of other assets being used on a continuing basis (other assets test).

> 💣 **Pitfall**
>
> If your taxable income after adding back investment losses plus any reportable fringe benefits and superannuation contributions is greater than $250 000, then the ATO will deny any business losses from being deductible in your tax return. This is regardless of whether or not you satisfy any of the non-commercial losses tests.

89 Franchising

If your business becomes quite successful you may toy with the thought of franchising it so that other people can pay you copious amounts of cash for your idea. Sounds really good in theory but you need excellent systems, patience and time to set it up properly.

Franchising is a highly complicated area with huge scope for franchisors to be sued by franchisees if you don't comply with the franchising laws correctly. It is strongly recommended that you hire expert franchising consultants to ensure that you get excellent advice in establishing the franchise correctly.

 Tip

Ensure that you have a new company to hold the intellectual property (IP) and another separate company from your original trading company to house the head franchisor. This structure will help protect your assets should the unthinkable occur.

According to the ATO, payments received from the franchisee — such as advertising costs, the initial franchise fee, service fees, royalties and training fees — will form part of the franchisor's assessable income for income tax purposes. As these payments are likely to be over $75 000 per annum the franchisor will need to register for GST and charge it accordingly. The franchisor will need to report and remit the GST to the ATO on a quarterly basis. If the franchisee is GST registered, they can claim a GST credit in their business activity statement for the GST paid to the franchisor.

 Pitfall

It can be very costly (as much as $250 000) to set up the correct franchising structure as well as complying with all of the requirements of the Franchising Code of Conduct administered through the Australian Competition and Consumer Commission (ACCC).

You also need to maintain a separate set of financial records for each company created in the structure, resulting in higher administration fees such as accounting, tax, audit and Australian Securities and Investments Commission annual return fees.

Part VIII

Miscellaneous

Wouldn't it be great if the tax system fitted nicely into seven parts? Unfortunately, tax legislation is wide and varied. And it will only continue to grow in years to come as the only constant with tax is change.

Part VIII looks at a few more concessions that are available to taxpayers as well as some of the administrative aspects of taxation such as lodgements, penalties, data matching and what to do if you have problems paying your tax debt. I'll also look at earning income overseas and tell you how to get a great accountant.

 Pitfall

While income-protection insurance is deductible, individuals cannot claim a tax deduction for life insurance. Life insurance is only deductible within super.

90 *Overseas income*

The tax treatment of foreign income by Australian tax residents can be complicated, particularly when foreign tax credits are added into the equation.

> **Tax fact**
>
> If you are an Australian resident, you are taxed on worldwide income. Any foreign income will need to be included in your tax return as assessable income and you may be entitled to a foreign income tax offset for amounts of foreign tax paid. Non-residents are only taxed on their Australian-sourced income.

The ATO considers you an Australian resident for tax purposes if you meet any of the following conditions:

▶ you are born and bred in Australia

▶ you are living permanently in Australia

▶ you have been living in Australia for at least six months and working the majority of that time at the same job and living at the same place

> **Proposed change**
>
> It was announced in the 2015–16 federal budget that effective from 1 January 2017 pensioners who have lived in Australia for fewer than 35 years will be paid a reduced pension proportional to their Australian working life residence ratio. This reduction will apply only when they are absent from Australia for at least six weeks.

▶ you have been living in Australia for more than half of the financial year, except where your usual home is overseas and you do not intend to live in Australia permanently.

If you are an Australian resident who is engaged in foreign service for a continuous period of 91 days or more you may be eligible for an exemption on Australian tax on this employment income if your employer:

▶ provides Australian official development assistance

▶ operates and maintains a public fund for disaster relief for people in a developing country

▶ is exempt from Australian income tax

▶ is an Australian Government authority that has deployed you outside Australia as a member of a disciplined force.

💣 Pitfall

If you have a foreign currency denominated bank account with a balance greater than A$250 000, you may be subject to Australian tax on any realised foreign currency gains or losses, even if you are merely depositing money and making withdrawals.

💣 Pitfall

If you think you don't need to declare your overseas income then think again. The ATO has tax treaties with 44 countries that allow them to exchange information about offshore income and transactions. Any data received is matched against Australian tax returns.

The ATO also receives information from the Australian Transaction Reports and Analysis Centre (AUSTRAC), which monitors domestic and international transactions over $10 000.

If you have been an Australian resident but you leave Australia, then you need to be aware that:

▶ you are still taxed in Australia on any Australian-sourced income

▶ any overseas assets are deemed to be disposed for capital gains tax purposes, potentially giving rise to a tax liability

▶ any HELP or SFSS debts will continue to be indexed.

 Proposed change

It was announced in the 2015 federal budget that from the 2016–17 income year, graduates living overseas and earning incomes above the minimum HELP repayment threshold (see p. 83) will be required to make repayments towards their HELP debts.

 Tip

If you move overseas and become a non-resident, notify your bank (regarding interest) and share registries (dividends), so that withholding tax is deducted at the source and you will have no further tax obligation in Australia for this income, including not needing to disclose it in your Australian tax return.

 Tip

If you have worked overseas and had retirement benefits paid on your behalf then consider transferring the balance of your foreign pension account to your complying Australian superannuation fund. (For more information, see p. 191.)

FAQ

Which figure do I record in my tax return with respect to foreign currency trading? The balance after losses taken out of profit or only the profit position?

You should be recording the net profit or loss, not just the profit only position. If the losses are greater than the gains then you will probably need to quarantine the losses to future years subject to the non-commercial losses rules.

91 Getting a great accountant

A friend once told me that there are two things in life that people need — a good mechanic and a great accountant.

Tip

A great accountant is just like a surveyor because they know where the boundaries are. They will ensure that you go to the limit with your deductions but that you don't claim so much that you leave yourself open to a visit from the ATO auditors. With their fees being tax-deductible too, why wouldn't you use a professional to handle your affairs?

Taxation is a complex area and deserves the attention of a specialist to give you the right advice to ensure you are maximising deductions yet staying within the regulations.

For some people, tax is a pain and they pay a small fee to get rid of the discomfort. But remember that if you pay peanuts, you get monkeys, so do not base your decision solely on price because a bad accountant could cost you thousands down the track due to a dodgy claim or missing a key strategy to save tax.

 Pitfall

You are not protected if a dodgy accountant claims deductions that you cannot substantiate. If you find an accountant who is dodgy, report them immediately to the authorities. We all hate paying tax, but if everyone pays their fair share then we can expect taxes to be lowered in the future.

The most important thing is to pick an accountant who is a registered tax agent and also a member of a professional body. This at least provides you with some confidence that they are educated and keep reasonably up to date each year with the changing tax laws.

There are three professionally recognised accountancy bodies in Australia:

▶ Institute of Chartered Accountants in Australia (ICAA) www.charteredaccountants.com.au

▶ CPA Australia www.cpaaustralia.com.au

▶ Institute of Public Accountants (IPA) www.publicaccountants.org.au

While it is nice to have an accountant who communicates well, it is more important that they are communicating the right information to you. Ask your friends for recommendations as they can report on their own experience. I also find that a well-constructed website with regular client newsletters and updates that are in plain, simple English is really important. Like mechanics, don't pick someone who treats you like a typical 'dumb' client but rather someone who takes the time to explain things in more depth.

Tax fact

According to the ATO, the average cost of managing tax affairs claimed by an individual in the 2012–13 financial year was $379.

Tip

A great accountant, like a top doctor, is likely to be busy so don't get frustrated if he or she cannot see you at the drop of a hat.

Picking someone who is located near your workplace or business will save you a lot of unnecessary travel time, but you would travel the earth for a great accountant.

Finally, trust your instincts. Your finances represent a hugely important matter, so give it the attention it requires. If you don't feel comfortable, find another accountant.

Tip

Always ask for a quote in advance of work being prepared by an accountant so you are not shocked when the bill arrives. Unexpected invoices have ended many a client–accountant relationship.

92 *Lodging your tax return*

It is compulsory to lodge your income tax return on time. Individuals have to lodge their returns by 31 October each year, unless they are lodging through a registered tax agent. Other entities such as companies, trusts, partnerships and super funds have different lodgement dates that the ATO advises.

☼ Tip

If you are having difficulties getting your tax return lodged by the deadline, or perhaps you have a tax liability, consider appointing a registered tax agent before 31 October. By going on their tax lodgement program you can defer lodging your tax return to 31 March, or even as late as 15 May for some taxpayers.

Registered tax agents get extremely busy around tax deadlines. While some will do anything to help you, including working around the clock, don't leave it to the last minute to see your tax agent as they may be too busy to help.

If you are comfortable with doing your own tax, you can prepare and lodge your tax return online with either e-tax or MyTax, the ATO's free tax return preparation software programs. MyTax is designed for taxpayers with simple tax affairs while e-tax is for more complicated returns. Refunds are generally issued within 12 business days. The software is usually available between 1 July and 31 May each financial year.

Tip

Steps to prepare your income tax return via e-tax:
1   Download the e-tax software from www.ato.gov.au/etax.
2   Verify your identity.
3   Complete your return using pre-filled information from employers, banks, share registries and others.
4   Check, save and print a copy for your records.
5   Lodge online and get an instance confirmation receipt.
6   Receive any refund due within 12 business days.

People who don't send in their tax return by the due date may be charged late-lodgement penalties or may even be prosecuted. Penalties for late lodgement of tax returns can be as high as $5000, as well as good behaviour bonds and jail sentences. From 1 July 2015, the late lodgement of business activity statements (BAS) incurs a fine of $180 for each month late, up to a maximum penalty of $900 per BAS.

Since 2014, the ATO now provides MyTax, an online pre-prepared tax return for people without complex tax affairs. Australian resident taxpayers will be able to use MyTax if they have income only from salary, wages, allowances, bank interest, dividends and/or Australian government payments. The only deductions allowed are for work-related expenses, expenses related to interest or dividend income, donations and/or the costs of managing their tax affairs, and the only offsets that can be claimed are the senior and pensioner tax offset and/or zone and overseas forces tax offset.

Tip

Steps to prepare your income tax return via MyTax:

1   Check your eligibility to use MyTax at www.ato.gov.au/MyTax.
2   Wait until the end of August for all information of wages, dividends and interest to filter in from employers, share registries and banks.
3   Register a MyGov account at www.my.gov.au.
4   Review the pre-filled return with information from employers, share registries, banks and private health companies.
5   Enter any missing details to complete your return.
6   Save and print a copy for your records.
7   Lodge online and get an instant confirmation receipt.
8   Receive any refund due within 12 business days.

 Tip

If your tax affairs are not basic (for example, you run a business or you sold some shares), then you use e-tax or a registered tax agent rather than MyTax.

While MyTax may be simple to use, ensure you do not rush yourself and miss out on claiming legitimate tax deductions for car, home office or any of the other tips contained in this book!

 Pitfall

While the pre-filling service provided by e-tax and MyTax is very helpful, do not rely on the information being 100 per cent accurate. The pre-filling report is rarely up to date in the July–August period as it takes time for employers, banks and share registries to send the relevant information to the ATO. Managed fund investments are notoriously late in reporting as well (usually October or November). If you didn't provide your TFN to one of these reporters then any income derived from these sources will not show up either. As the onus is on you to accurately report your taxable income, double check the pre-filling report against your records prior to lodgement.

93 *Amending returns and objecting to assessments*

Amendments

Whether it is missed interest income or a deduction that you forgot to claim, it is possible to lodge a request with the ATO to amend your income tax return, even long after your original return was lodged and assessed. Generally the ATO has the power to amend returns for up to four years after lodgement of the original return.

Bonus resources

If you need to amend your tax return you can download and complete the ATO form *Request for amendment of income tax return for individuals* (NAT 2843-10.2010) from the ATO website.

If you have made a mistake or need to amend your tax return, it is important you do so promptly. You can either download the ATO amendment request form or send a letter to the ATO (PO Box 3004, Penrith NSW 2740).

Tip

If you wish to amend your tax return, ensure your amendment request letter contains the following information:

▶ your name, address and contact phone number
▶ your TFN
▶ the income tax year that the amendment relates to
▶ the reason for the amendment of the return
▶ the item number of the tax return that requires amendment
▶ the amount of the amendment
▶ a declaration that all the information provided, including any attachments, is true and correct and that you have the necessary receipts and other records to support your claim for amendment.

You will also need to sign and date the letter.

 Pitfall

If the amendment of your income tax return results in extra tax required to be paid, the ATO will charge you interest penalties but generally will reduce any other penalties if you have voluntarily told them in advance of any potential audit activity by them of your error.

Objections

If the ATO issues you with a notice of assessment that you disagree with, you don't have to simply 'like it or lump it'. You generally have up to two years to submit an objection to your assessment with the ATO. If you are objecting to an ATO ruling, other than an assessment, then you generally have only 60 days to lodge your objection to their decision.

All objections must be in writing and signed and dated. You can either download the ATO objection form or send a letter to the ATO (PO Box 1130, Penrith NSW 2740). The ATO generally take eight weeks to make a decision about your objection. If you disagree with that decision then you can apply for an independent external review.

Ensure that your objection letter includes the following:

▶ your name, address and contact phone number

▶ your TFN

▶ the income tax year that the amendment relates to

▶ the reasons why you think that the ATO's original decision is wrong

▶ the relevant facts, arguments, information and documents that support the reasons you disagree with the ATO decision (including legislation, case law and rulings)

▶ a declaration that all the information provided, including any attachments, is true and correct

▶ any supporting documents and information that relates to the decision being reviewed.

Tax fact

Since 1 July 2014, the ATO has issued most individual taxpayers with a tax receipt in conjunction with the original notice of assessment as part of the annual income tax return process.

The tax receipt contains a table showing how your taxes have been allocated to key categories of government expenditure. It also includes information on the level of Australian Government gross debt for the current and previous years.

Bonus resources

If you want to lodge an objection you can download and complete the ATO form *Object form—for taxpayers* (NAT 13471) from the ATO website.

🔆 **Tip**

You cannot formally object to the following:

▶ a general interest charge (GIC)
▶ a shortfall interest charge
▶ a late lodgement penalty.

However, you can still talk to the ATO if you disagree with their decision. The ATO will review your file and determine if those charges are still applicable.

 94 *ATO data matching*

Over the past five years, data matching has been a powerful tax compliance tool for the ATO. It has acted as a huge deterrent for taxpayers thinking about not disclosing all of their income.

Tax fact

In 2013–14 the ATO recovered an extra $951.6 million in adjustments after reviewing more than 650 million transactions and conducting over 480 000 data matching reviews.

When you lodge your income tax return, the onus is firmly on you to make sure that the information contained within the return is complete and correct.

 Tip

Don't try to understate any of your income. If you are on the tax lodgement program of a registered tax agent, then they will generally get a pre-filling report from the ATO to help identify income you may otherwise have missed. It takes time for this information to filter through from the relevant institutions, so the report needs to be seen as a starting point for doing your tax return, not a comprehensive solution.

The ATO has a responsibility to the community to ensure that everyone pays their fair share of tax under the law. If all taxes are correctly collected it means better roads, hospitals and education and perhaps even lower taxes as well. The ATO checks taxpayer compliance with the law by verifying the amounts included in tax returns with information from third parties.

The ATO gets its hands on data from a number of institutions, including the following:

▶ AUSTRAC, which provides information on banking transactions over $10 000

▶ Australian Securities and Investments Commission (ASIC)

▶ banks, financial institutions and investment bodies, which provide investment income information such as interest, dividends and managed funds

▶ Centrelink

▶ Child Support Registrar

▶ credit card and debit card transactions for all merchants with a turnover of less than $10 million

► Department of Immigration and Citizenship

► employers, who provide employment information including PAYG payment summaries

► industry bodies, which provide information for specific transactions

► Medicare Australia, which provides data that enables it to administer the health insurance incentives rebate

► motor registries, which provide information on individuals and entities that have purchased motor vehicles valued over $10 000

► share registries, which provide information on share transactions for CGT purposes

► state and territory revenue offices, which provide information on house purchases and disposals

► suppliers, which provide purchase information of purchases greater than a certain amount

► 34 foreign governments that have signed tax information exchange agreements with Australia.

Tax fact

Since 1 July 2013, businesses in the building and construction industry need to report the total payments they make to each contractor for building and construction services each year.

The ATO then matches this data with information lodged in tax returns to detect those who may not be showing all of their income correctly in their tax returns. If there are any discrepancies the ATO will take further action, which may include audits, penalties and, in some cases, imprisonment. Industry-wide data is also analysed (and benchmarking exercises are conducted) to identify trends and to allow the ATO to focus on future compliance risks.

 Pitfall

As pressure on tax collection has increased in recent years, so too has ATO audit activity. In the past few years, the tax man has requested personal information from eBay and the Trading Post Australia on those users who have sold goods or services greater than $20 000 in any of the past three financial years.

The ATO also identifies people who have never paid taxes or who are behind in lodging tax returns and activity statements, paying taxes or meeting their employer superannuation obligations.

95 *Problems paying your tax*

You must pay your tax as and when it falls due. But there are times when you simply cannot pay your tax and BAS obligations on time. If you are in this situation contact the ATO immediately to discuss your circumstances. ATO officers are very understanding of your situation and will be as fair and reasonable as possible with you.

 Tip

Don't delay the lodgement of your outstanding tax and BAS returns simply because you don't have the money to pay, because there are penalties for late lodgement too.

It is likely that you will need to provide the ATO with your true financial position (such as a list of assets, liabilities, income and expenditure) to show that you are having difficulties meeting your debts as and when they fall due. Depending on your individual circumstances, you may be given an extension of time to pay the ATO.

Pitfall

If you get an extension of time to pay your taxes, the ATO will impose a general interest charge (GIC), which accrues on your debt until it is paid off in full. The GIC, currently 9.36 per cent, is tax-deductible in the financial year in which it is charged.

Along with meeting your monthly repayments, you will need to ensure that any future tax returns and activity statements are lodged and paid on time. Failure to do so will be considered a default on your payment arrangement, and will require an explanation to the ATO.

Tax fact

If you operate a small business and are struggling to manage your tax-payment obligations you may be able to request a 12-month GIC-free payment arrangement from the ATO, and you may also be able to defer your activity statement payment due dates.

Depending on your individual circumstances, the ATO has the ability to release you from some or all of your tax debts. If paying your tax would cause you 'serious hardship' by preventing you from providing the basic necessities (such as food, shelter, clothing and education) for yourself and your family, then you may apply for this concession.

Taxpayers in this situation will need to complete an 'application for release' form and provide supporting documentation showing how payment of the tax debt will cause serious hardship.

Bonus resources

If you would like to be granted a release for some or all of your debt you can complete the ATO's *Application for release* form (NAT 15080).

96 *Medical expenses tax offset*

It doesn't pay to get sick, particularly as doctors and medications are not cheap these days.

However, to help you with paying your costs you can claim, via your tax return, a rebate of 20 per cent of your net medical expenses (including those medical expenses of your dependants) for the amounts incurred over $2162 in a financial year.

Tax fact

For taxpayers with an adjusted taxable income above the Medicare levy surcharge thresholds ($90 000 for singles and $180 000 for couples or families), the threshold above which a taxpayer may claim the medical expenses offset increases to $5100 (indexed annually). The rebate will be reduced to 10 per cent for eligible out-of-pocket expenses incurred.

The medical expenses tax offset covers 'the gap' that you pay after any refunds from Medicare or your private health fund. The expenses must be related to an illness or operation provided by a registered medical practitioner, including payments to doctors, nurses, dentists, orthodontists, opticians and optometrists. It also includes medical aids, medicines and therapeutic treatments prescribed by a doctor.

 Pitfall

The net medical expenses tax offset is being gradually phased out. Taxpayers can only claim the medical expenses tax offset in 2014–15 if they received the offset in the preceding year (pending having net expenses above the relevant thresholds). The offset will continue to be available for out-of-pocket medical expenses relating to disability aids, attendant or aged care until 1 July 2019.

FAQ

Can I claim the medical expenses tax offset for those expenses that have been funded by the NDIS?

Unfortunately you cannot include net medical expenses that have been funded by the NDIS. However, if you incur additional medical expenses that you pay for out of your own pocket then you may be eligible to claim this tax offset.

Example

Joe incurs medical expenses of $4000 for the 2013–14 financial year. He received $450 back from Medicare and a further $550 from his private health fund. In his tax return he can claim a rebate of $167.60, which is 20 per cent of his net medical expenses over $2162.

Tip

If you have already reached your $2162 threshold in a financial year you may want to bring forward some medical costs prior to 30 June so that you effectively get a 20 per cent discount when you claim the offset in your tax return.

The ATO allows medical expenses for the following payments:

▶ artificial limbs or eyes

▶ hearing aids

▶ a carer who looks after a person who is blind or permanently confined to a bed or wheelchair

▶ registered dental mechanics

▶ laser eye surgery

▶ maintaining a properly trained dog for guiding or assisting people with a disability

▶ medical expenses incurred overseas

▶ therapeutic treatment under the direction of a doctor

▶ in-vitro fertilisation (IVF) treatments

▶ prescriptions (including prescribed medical aids)

▶ prescription spectacles and contact lenses.

You can generally get an itemised annual statement from the following organisations to help you reconstruct your expenses:

▶ Medicare

▶ your private health fund

▶ pharmacies where you get your subscriptions.

💣 **Pitfall**

The ATO will not allow expenses for the following payments for the medical expenses tax offset:

- ▶ ambulance
- ▶ chemist-type items that are available on the shelf in retail outlets and health food stores, such as tablets for pain relief
- ▶ private health insurance
- ▶ cosmetic surgery for which a Medicare benefit is not payable
- ▶ travel inoculations
- ▶ medical examinations for life insurance purposes
- ▶ funeral expenses
- ▶ non-prescribed vitamins or health foods
- ▶ purchases from a chemist that are not related to an illness or operation
- ▶ therapeutic treatment where the patient is not formally referred by a doctor
- ▶ travel and accommodation expenses associated with medical treatment.

97 *Levies*

Medicare levy surcharge

For more than 25 years, the Medicare scheme has provided Australians with greater access to health care. It has been funded by a Medicare levy paid by individual taxpayers who are also Australian residents. The levy is charged by the ATO based on 2 per cent of your taxable income via your notice of assessment each year.

Tax fact

The Medicare levy was raised on 1 July 2014 by half a percentage point to 2 per cent to provide a funding stream for DisabilityCare Australia. The money raised from the increase is being placed into a DisabilityCare Australia Fund for 10 years, which will only be drawn upon to fund the additional costs of delivering the NDIS.

If you or your dependants do not have private health insurance and your 'adjusted taxable income' was above a certain amount, you may have to pay an additional Medicare levy surcharge on top of the standard 2 per cent levy.

Pitfall

If you are over 30 and don't have private health cover there are lifetime health cover penalties that apply when you subsequently take out cover. For each year over age 30 that you delay in getting basic hospital cover, you will have to pay an extra 2 per cent on your premium, up to a maximum of 70 per cent, when you finally take out the cover.

The Medicare levy surcharge is an additional levy of up to 1.5 per cent, charged on your adjusted taxable income, which is the sum of:

▶ your taxable income

▶ your reportable super contributions

▶ your net investment losses

▶ your total reportable fringe benefits

▶ any amount on which family trust distribution tax has been paid.

Tip

The size of your Medicare levy surcharge is affected by your level of income, your marital status, the number of children you have and your age, as outlined in tables 8.1 and 8.2. If you earn more than the adjusted taxable income threshold, take out basic hospital cover to avoid the Medicare levy surcharge, as it will probably be cheaper.

If you and your dependants have private health insurance, you may be eligible for a refundable tax rebate. It can be received as a refund even if you do not have to pay any tax. Similar to the Medicare levy surcharge, this private health rebate is affected by your income, marital status and age.

Table 8.1: Medicare levy surcharge and private health insurance rebate (singles) (2015–16)

Adjusted taxable income	Medicare levy surcharge	Rebate if under age 65	Rebate if aged 65–69 years	Rebate if over age 70
Up to $90 000	Nil	27.82%	32.457%	37.094%
$90 001–$105 000	1%	18.547%	23.184%	27.820%
$105 001– $140 000	1.25%	9.273%	13.910%	18.547%
over $140 000	1.5%	0%	0%	0%

Source: © Australian Taxation Office for the Commonwealth of Australia.

Table 8.2: Medicare levy surcharge and private health insurance rebate (couples or single parents) (2015–16)

Adjusted taxable income (total)*	Medicare levy surcharge	Rebate if under age 65	Rebate if aged 65–69 years	Rebate if over age 70
Up to $180 000	Nil	27.82%	32.457%	37.094%
$180 001–$210 000	1%	18.547%	23.184%	27.820%
$210 001–$280 000	1.25%	9.273%	13.910%	18.547%
Over $280 000	1.5%	0%	0%	0%

*The threshold rises by $1500 for each dependent child born after the first.

Source: © Australian Taxation Office for the Commonwealth of Australia.

 Tip

If you know that you are going to fall above a higher income threshold (or you are unsure what your income level will be), then contact your private health provider at the start of the year and reduce the rebate that you receive upfront. Otherwise you might get a nasty surprise when you get your tax assessment and find out that you have to pay back a part or all of your rebate that you were not entitled to receive.

 Pitfall

It was announced in the 2014–15 federal budget that the income thresholds used to calculate the Medicare levy surcharge and private health insurance rebate will not be adjusted for three years and will remain at the 2014–15 levels for 2015–16, 2016–17 and 2017–18.

(continued)

Pitfall *(cont'd)*

Those with incomes just below each threshold may move above a higher income threshold if their income increases (known as 'bracket creep'). For those with private health insurance, your rebate percentage entitlement may decrease. For those that do not have the appropriate level of private patient hospital cover, you may have to pay either the Medicare levy surcharge or if you paid the surcharge in the previous year, the rate of the surcharge may increase.

 Tip

Consider prepaying up to 12 months of private medical cover before the end of the current tax year if you think your taxable income in the subsequent financial year will take you above one of the private health insurance rebate 'income thresholds' in table 8.1 (singles) and table 8.2 (couples). The situation might arise if you are planning on realising a large capital gain or perhaps receiving a big bonus after 30 June. By implementing this strategy you will be able to get the higher rebate percentage back to you in the current year.

Temporary budget repair levy

It was announced in the 2014–15 federal budget that a 2 per cent levy would be introduced for the excess taxable income above $180 000 for three years from 1 July 2014. In addition to the increase in the Medicare levy by half a percentage point to 2 per cent, this means that the highest marginal tax rate has effectively jumped from 46.5 per cent to 49 per cent for the 2014–15, 2015–16 and 2016–17 financial years.

98 *Zone and overseas forces tax offsets*

If you lived or worked in a remote area or served in forces overseas during the financial year you may be able to claim a tax offset.

Zone tax offset

This is often a forgotten claim—particularly if you use an accountant outside of the region where you live. The offset is available if you lived in a remote or isolated part of Australia, not including an offshore oil or gas rig, for at least half of the financial year.

> **Tax fact**
>
> The ATO classifies remote areas into two zones—zone A and zone B —and designates special areas within these zones. If you are unsure whether you are in a remote area, the ATO has an Australian zone list available on its website.

To qualify for the zone tax offset, you must have worked or lived in a remote area for 183 days or more during the current financial year or, if you haven't previously claimed the zone tax offset, 183 days or more in total during the current and previous financial years—but less than 183 days in the current year and less than 183 days in the previous financial year.

Note that the time spent in a remote area does not have to be continuous.

Proposed change

It was proposed in the 2015 federal budget that effective 1 July 2015, 'fly-in fly-out' and 'drive-in drive-out' workers will cease to be eligible for the zone tax offset when their normal residence is not within a zone.

 Pitfall

Some tax agents who live in capital cities do not automatically think of this tax offset, so it is wise to prompt them if you do live in a zone area.

Overseas forces tax offset

If you have served during the financial year in a specified overseas locality as a member of either the Australian defence forces or the United Nations forces, and your income relating to that service was not specifically exempt from tax, you may be eligible for an overseas forces tax offset.

 Tip

You can only claim for either the overseas forces tax offset or the zone tax offset in your income tax return, even if you qualify for both. So pick the one that gives the higher claim.

To claim the full overseas forces tax offset, you must have served in one or more overseas localities for 183 days or more during the financial year. A portion of the offset may still be claimed even if your overseas service was fewer than 183 days.

The tax offset amounts are shown in table 8.3.

Table 8.3: zone and overseas forces tax offsets (2014–15)

Your circumstances	Zone A	Zone B	Special area	Overseas forces
You were single with no dependent child or student for whole of year	$338	$57	$1173	$338
You are able to claim the maximum dependant (invalid and carer) tax offset ($2535)	$1615	$566	$2471	$1615

Source: © Australian Taxation Office for the Commonwealth of Australia.

 ## *Tax-effective investments*

Around May and June each year, there are a number of accountants and financial planners who try to promote tax-effective investments in agribusiness and forestry products.

 Tip

A good financial adviser will recommend that you have no more than 5 per cent of your investment portfolio in tax-effective investments, given the high risk associated with them.

The ATO has labelled these investments as 'aggressive tax planning' products and for good reason—these investments have copped a lot of bad press in recent years thanks to some projects going into administration, resulting in their investors losing potentially thousands of dollars.

Tax fact

Investments in agribusiness or forestry products generally have 100 per cent tax-deductibility in the first year. Different from investments in shares or properties, if you invest say $100 000 in these types of investments you may get a tax deduction of $100 000.

☀ **Tip**

Before you sign up to any tax-effective scheme, ensure that there is a product ruling for the project issued by the ATO so that you can get some certainty on the tax benefits contained within the product disclosure statement.

Used the right way, they can be a very good tax-planning strategy; for example, they can help level out the tax on any capital gains or bonus during a financial year.

But sometimes these investments sound too good to be true. Potential investors must form their own view about the commercial and financial viability of the product. Take care before you invest because while you are getting a tax deduction you are still risking the amount not covered by your marginal tax rate. If the project doesn't generate its projected returns, you will be out of pocket after tax.

Pitfall

A product ruling issued by the ATO in no way guarantees the actual project, or whether it is even commercially viable. The ATO does not verify that the projected returns will be achieved or are reasonably based.

If the project is ultimately not carried out as described to the ATO originally, investors may also lose the protection of the tax benefits outlined in the product ruling.

100 *Tax planning as a 365-day process*

It always surprises me when people think that tax planning only occurs in June each year. Well, it may for those who are not very organised. But if you want to save as much as legitimately possible on your largest expense, I encourage you to start tax planning on the first day of July each year.

Throughout this book there are tips that are probably more applicable for action at the start of the year than at the end of the year.

 Tip

Tax planning should be a 365-day per year exercise, not one merely carried out in the last few weeks before 30 June. A lot of these strategies are just as useful on 1 July as they are on 30 June.

For example, a strategy such as super co-contribution is a lot more manageable if you take out $20 per week over a year, rather than trying to find $1000 at the end of the year.

For wealthier people, there is an opportunity at the start of each year to have a regular amount of each month's salary sacrificed into superannuation so that you take advantage of the concessionally taxed contribution limits.

Negative gearing and depreciation have much more impact when spread over a whole year rather than just a few days. A logbook is the best way of maximising your car deductions for work-related purposes but you can't just do one on 30 June—it takes 12 weeks of diligence in keeping accurate records.

 Pitfall

Tax agents cannot wave a magic wand if you don't do the basics and keep your receipts throughout the year for your work- or business-related expenses. The ATO's rule in most circumstances is that no receipt results in no deduction.

 Tip

Don't spend purely to get a tax deduction. Many people get suckered in by the sneaky marketing methods of retailers to buy items that are 'fully tax-deductible'. Remember that it is a play on marginal tax rates. Even if you are on the highest marginal tax rate, you are only getting a maximum of 49 per cent back. If you want a $50 000 tax deduction before 30 June I will gladly invoice you and accept payment. But you will only get a fraction back as a tax benefit and the transaction has reduced your bank balance and will affect cash flow. Always think of my ABC motto—Absolute Bloody Cash.

Tip

Before you make a donation to charity, check that they have deductible gift recipient (DGR) status, otherwise you will not be able to claim the deduction in your return.

101 *Just do it!*

Over the past few hundred pages you have read some great strategies to save money on your taxes — legally. Now it is time to take action.

 Tip

I am a big fan of the famous Nike advertising campaign. When you get great advice then 'Just Do It'. I get really annoyed when my clients don't follow through because they forgot or were too lazy to get around to it.

Thank you for taking the time to read this book. I hope it has been of benefit to you. Over time, I have no doubt that these strategies will save you significant amounts of money — and during tough times, every single dollar counts!

Tax fact

As mentioned in the introduction, not every single tip outlined in this book is applicable to everyone. But I guarantee you that at least one of these tips will save you more than the cost of this book. In fact, the purchase of this book as reference material for your tax affairs will be tax-deductible. Do you still have that receipt?

You will be surprised how many slackos there are that miss out on easy money despite how simple some of these strategies are. Take the superannuation co-contribution, for example.

If you procrastinated every year since the introduction of super co-contribution in 2003 (and there are a lot of people out there who have) and kept on forgetting to contribute post-tax dollars into super, you have missed out on over $10000 of free money from the government and the possibility that your retirement savings could be almost $20000 higher as well.

 Tip

The simplest way to remind yourself to action something is to put a follow-up reminder in your calendar. If you have a computer with an online calendar, such as the one in Microsoft Outlook, you can set up reminders on a regular basis as 'new appointments'. When the reminder pops up on your screen in the future, don't 'dismiss' until you have actioned it. Press 'snooze' instead.

 Pitfall

Research has found that 100 per cent of action plans that are not started result in the goals set out in the action plans not being achieved.

Can you and your family afford to miss out on this amount of money simply by leaving things to next week or next year?

I wish you and your family much happiness and hope that life is not too taxing!

Glossary

$1000 upfront tax concession If you acquire ESS interests under a taxed-upfront scheme that meets certain conditions, you will be eligible to receive a tax concession of up to $1000 if your taxable income after adjustments is $180 000 or less.

30-day rule If you dispose of your ESS interest within 30 days after the deferred taxing point, the deferred taxing point becomes the date of that disposal.

45-day rule See *holding period rule.*

ABN Australian business number; a unique identifying number issued to all entities registered in the Australian Business Register.

ABR Australian Business Register; the extensive database of identity information provided by businesses when they register for an ABN www.abr.gov.au.

ACCC   Australian Competition and Consumer Commission; government organisation responsible for ensuring compliance with the *Trade Practices Act 1974* www.accc.gov.au.

accruals basis   If you account for an invoice but do not receive the cash, you are using an accruals basis of accounting; you can use the cash basis if your annual turnover is $1 million or less.

adjusted taxable income   The sum of:

▶ taxable income

▶ reportable fringe benefits

▶ reportable superannuation contributions

▶ total net investment loss.

allowable deduction   An expense you can deduct from your assessable income.

APRA   Australian Prudential Regulation Authority—APRA is responsible for regulating certain types of super funds www.apra.gov.au.

ASIC   Australian Securities & Investments Commission — the corporate, markets and financial services regulator in Australia www.asic.gov.au.

assessable income   The income you derive, before deducting allowable deductions, that is liable to tax.

associate   Associates include people and entities closely associated with you, such as relatives, or closely connected companies or trustees of a trust (other than the trustee of an employee share trust). For example, a partner in a partnership is an associate of the partnership and an individual's spouse is an associate of the individual. You may also be an associate of a self managed super fund in which you are a member or a family trust of which you are a beneficiary.

ASX Australian Securities Exchange — the marketplace for trading shares, bonds and other securities in Australia www.asx.com.au.

ATO Australian Taxation Office — the ATO's role is to manage and collect tax as well as act as regulator of self managed super funds in Australia www.ato.gov.au.

AUSTRAC Australian Transaction Reports and Analysis Centre — Australia's anti–money laundering and counter-terrorism financing regulator and specialist financial intelligence unit www.austrac.gov.au.

BAS Business activity statement — a statement under the pay-as-you-go system that you prepare at the end of each quarter to remit GST, PAYG withholding and PAYG instalments.

beneficiary A person who is potentially entitled to a payment from a trust.

bonus shares Free shares issued by a company usually in proportion to your current share holdings.

brokerage fee The fee charged by a stockbroker when you buy or sell shares.

business real property A property that is used wholly or exclusively by one or more businesses.

buy contract note An invoice you receive from a stockbroker at the time you buy shares. It will summarise the details of the transaction and can be used to calculate a capital gain or capital loss for taxation purposes.

call option The right, but not the obligation, to buy the underlying shares at an agreed price on or before the date of expiration.

capital expenditure Money spent on assets like plant and equipment, goodwill, buildings, patents and copyrights.

capital loss The loss you incur when you sell CGT assets such as shares for a price that's below their reduced cost base; under Australian tax law a capital loss can only be offset against a capital gain.

capital protection loan A loan to buy shares where you can protect yourself from incurring a loss if your share portfolio falls in value.

cash basis If you issue (or receive) an invoice but do not account for the sale (or purchase) until the cash is received (or paid), you are using a cash basis of accounting; you can use the cash basis if your annual turnover is $1 million or less.

CCB Child care benefit—government benefit that helps eligible families with the cost of child care.

cents per kilometre method One of the four methods of claiming a deduction for car expenses. You can use this method up to a maximum of 5000 business kilometres. See table 2.1 on p. 39.

CGT Capital gains tax—the tax payable on the disposal of an investment asset that was acquired after 19 September 1985. It is not a separate tax, just part of your income tax. The most common way you make a capital gain (or capital loss) is by selling or disposing of assets such as real estate, shares or managed fund investments.

CGT asset register A register you keep to record all CGT assets you own, such as your share portfolio.

CGT event Normally arises when there's a change in ownership of a CGT asset.

company A separate legal entity, registered by ASIC, that can carry on a business in its own name; a company raises capital through the issue of shares.

company tax rate Currently 30 per cent of a company's taxable income (proposed to decrease to 28.5 per cent for small companies from 1 July 2015).

complying super fund A super fund that is regulated by the ATO and has been issued with a notice of compliance; complying funds that meet the *SIS Act 1993* standards qualify for a concessional tax rate.

concessional tax rate Super funds that comply with the *SIS Act 1993* qualify for the concessional tax rate of 15 per cent; non-complying super funds do not receive the concessional tax rate and are taxed at 45 per cent. Contributions made by individuals earning more than $300 000 are taxed at 30 per cent.

condition of release A condition, normally retirement, that must be satisfied before you can access your benefits in a superannuation fund.

contribution The money or asset directly contributed by an individual, an employer or another party into a super fund.

cost base The cost base of an asset is generally what it costs you. It is made up of five elements:

▶ the money you paid or property you gave for the asset

▶ the incidental costs of acquiring or selling it (for example, brokerage and stamp duty)

▶ costs of owning it (generally this will not apply to shares because you will usually have claimed or be entitled to claim these costs as tax deductions)

▶ costs associated with increasing or preserving its value, or with installing or moving it

▶ the cost to you to preserve or defend your title or rights to it.

CPA Australia One of the three professionally recognised accounting bodies in Australia (along with ICAA and IPA) www.cpaaustralia.com.au.

CPI Consumer price index—the general inflation index prepared by the Australian Bureau of Statistics that measures the change in the price of a fixed basket of goods bought by households.

crystallise To dispose of shares in order to create or realise a capital gain or capital loss.

dad and partner pay Government benefit paid to the father of the newborn child (or partner of the birth parent) to help with costs after the birth of the baby. The pay is for up to two weeks at the minimum wage, and is taxable.

deferred taxing point The earliest of the following times:

▶ seven years after you acquired a share/right

▶ the time you cease the employment in respect of which you acquired the share/right

▶ the time when there is no real risk of forfeiture and the scheme no longer genuinely restricts the disposal of the share/right.

dependants People you look after who need your financial support; usually spouse and minor children.

depreciation A non-cash expense which is the decline in value of an asset over time.

derived Income you earn that is liable for tax.

DGR Deductible gift recipient.

DICTO Dependant (invalid and carer) tax offset— available to taxpayers who maintain a dependant who is genuinely unable to work due to carer obligation or disability. In this instance, eight dependency tax offsets have been consolidated into a single, streamlined and non-refundable offset.

DIDO Drive-in drive-out—an arrangement where the employee drives a considerable distance from/to their normal residence to work for a number of days on a regular and rotational basis, and has a number of days of that are not the same days in consecutive weeks. Special LAFHA rules apply.

directors   Appointed by shareholders to manage and run the day-to-day operations of a company.

DisabilityCare Australia   The national disability insurance scheme funded by an increase in the Medicare levy (to 2 per cent) from 1 July 2014.

discounted capital gain   A 50 per cent reduction on the capital gain on disposal of CGT assets that were owned for at least 12 months.

discretionary trust   A trust where the trustee has discretion as to how the trust net income should be distributed to the beneficiaries.

dividend   A distribution of profit paid to shareholders of a company in proportion to the number of shares owned.

dividend reinvestment plan   A scheme where a company gives shareholders the option of reinvesting dividends in the form of new shares in the company, rather than receiving the dividends in cash.

DIY super   Do-it-yourself superannuation, also known as an SMSF.

DRP   Dividend reinvestment plan.

election   When a taxpayer makes a choice, usually in writing, with respect to adopting a certain tax law ahead of another.

ESS   Employee share scheme; a scheme under which shares, stapled securities and rights (including options) to acquire shares and stapled securities in a company are provided to its employees (including current, past or prospective employees and their associates) in relation to their employment.

ESS interests   Shares, stapled securities, or rights (including options) to acquire shares or stapled securities.

ESS statement   An annual statement that shows an estimate of any discounts you or your associates have received on your ESS interests.

e-tax   The ATO's online tax preparation program for self-preparers with tax affairs that are too complex to use MyTax www.ato.gov.au/etax.

ETP   Employment termination payment (previously known as an eligible termination payment); a lump-sum payment made due to your employment being terminated.

family discretionary trust   A trust whose membership is ordinarily made up of family beneficiaries; the trustee has discretion to distribute trust net income to certain beneficiaries.

FBT   Fringe benefits tax.

FHSA   First home saver accounts.

FIFO   Fly-in fly-out—an arrangement where the employee flies from/to their normal residence to work for a number of days on a regular and rotational basis and has a number of days off that are not the same days in consecutive weeks. Special LAFHA rules apply.

financial year   The period from 1 July to 30 June the following year.

foreign tax credit   Foreign tax paid on income derived from overseas sources that can be offset against Australian tax payable on taxable income derived from worldwide sources.

franked dividends   Dividends paid by an Australian resident company from profits that have had Australian company tax paid on them.

franking credits The amounts of tax paid previously by a company that are allocated to dividends paid to shareholders; the taxpayer receives the credits in their income tax assessment to avoid double taxation; also known as imputation credits.

GIC General interest charge — interest rate imposed by the ATO for late payment of tax.

GST Goods and services tax — 10 per cent tax on goods and services.

HELP Higher Education Loan Program.

holding period rule The rule where shareholders must continuously hold shares 'at risk' for at least 45 days (90 days for preference shares) around the ex-dividend date in order to be eligible for the franking tax offset. However, under the small shareholder exemption, this rule does not apply if your total franking credit entitlement is below $5000, which is roughly equivalent to receiving a fully franked dividend of $11 666 (based on the current tax rate of 30 per cent for companies).

IAS Instalment activity statement — a statement under the pay-as-you-go system that you prepare at the end of each reporting period disclosing certain income that is liable to tax.

ICAA Institute of Chartered Accountants in Australia — one of the three professionally recognised accounting bodies in Australia (along with CPA Australia and IPA) www.charteredaccountants.com.au.

imputation credit See *franking credits*.

income tax A federal tax that you pay on taxable income you derive.

income tax return Annual form lodged with the ATO disclosing your taxable income.

incurred The point in time when you can legally claim a deduction, usually when you have a commitment and a legal obligation to make a payment for certain goods and services you receive.

indeterminate right   A right to acquire at a future time either:

▶   shares or cash (at the discretion of your employer)

▶   a number of shares, where that number cannot be determined at the time of acquisition of the right but will be determined at a later time.

initial repairs   Costs to rectify damage, defects or deterioration that existed at the time of purchasing a property and considered to be capital in nature and not deductible for tax purposes.

instalment warrant   A form of derivative or financial product that entails borrowing to invest in an underlying asset, such as a share or real property, with limited risk to the investor. The underlying asset is held in trust during the life of the loan to provide limited security for the lender. The investor is required to pay one or more future instalments to the lender.

investment strategy   A document setting out how you intend to invest your benefits in an SMSF; it must be in writing and must consider investment risks, the likely returns and whether you have sufficient cash on hand to discharge liabilities when they fall due.

IP   Intellectual property.

IPA   IPA Institute of Public Accountants, formerly National Institute of Accountants — one of the three professionally recognised accounting bodies in Australia (along with ICAA and CPA Australia) www.publicaccountants.org.au.

ITAA 1936   *The Income Tax Assessment Act 1936.*

ITAA 1997   *The Income Tax Assessment Act 1997.*

LAFHA Living-away-from-home allowance — a tax-free allowance paid to employees who are required to perform their work duties away from their usual place of residence.

LITO Low-income tax offset.

LMR Lost members register — a register maintained by the ATO showing a list of lost and unclaimed super.

low-income tax offset A general tax offset you can claim if your taxable income is below a certain threshold; the tax offset is reduced by 1.5 cents for every dollar you earn above the threshold.

low-value pool A pool of depreciable assets, each with a written-down value under $1000, which can be depreciated at a more favourable pool rate of 37.5 per cent per annum.

margin call The shortfall required if the value of your shares, funded by a margin loan, falls below a certain level.

margin loan A form of borrowing to fund a share portfolio.

marginal tax rate The rate of tax applicable to the last dollar of your taxable income; your average tax rate on your entire taxable income is generally lower than your marginal tax rate.

Medicare levy A 2 per cent levy charged on your taxable income.

Medicare levy surcharge An extra levy (up to 1.5 per cent) charged on taxable income when taxpayers do not have private health insurance and their 'adjusted taxable income' is above a certain amount.

MyTax The ATO's online tax preparation program for self-preparers with simple tax affairs www.ato.gov.au/MyTax.

NDIS (National Disability Insurance Scheme) Tax-exempt assistance received by eligible people with a disability

negative gearing   Occurs when the net rental income from an investment property, after deducting other expenses, is less than the interest on the borrowings, a very popular tax strategy employed by Australians; these properties are purchased with the assistance of borrowed funds and partly repaid by the tax benefits subsequently received.

non-complying super fund   A super fund that is not residing in Australia or that has been issued with a notice of non-compliance because it does not comply with the *SIS Act 1993*; non-complying super funds do not receive the concessional tax rate and are taxed at 45 per cent.

non-resident   a person who does not normally reside in Australia and has no intention of living here; a non-resident is liable to pay tax only on income sourced in Australia. People who are temporarily in Australia for a working holiday are treated as non-residents for tax purposes, regardless of how long they are here.

notice of compliance   The ATO will issue this notice if it makes a determination that a fund complies with the *SIS Act 1993*; the determination is only made after an SMSF annual return has been lodged with the ATO.

objection   A formal challenge against an ATO assessment or decision.

option   An option is a form of right: if you receive an option, you make an agreement with the provider of the option, allowing you to buy shares or stapled securities during a certain time period, for a particular price (the exercise price); you then have the right, but not the obligation, to exercise the option.

paid parental leave   Government benefit paid to a parent of a newborn child to help care for the baby; the pay is for up to 18 weeks at the minimum wage and is taxable.

partnership   Two or more people in business with a common view to making a profit.

PAYG (pay-as-you-go) withholding the tax deducted from an employee's wages by an employer and remitted to the ATO.

PAYG withholding variation application a form, which is virtually a mini tax return, that estimates your taxable income for the upcoming year to reduce the tax deducted from your pay packet.

pension age the age used to determine eligibility for certain government benefits, including the age pension; the pension age is currently 65 but proposed to increase to 67 in 2023 and 70 by 2035.

positive gearing the opposite of negative gearing; it occurs when the net rental income from an investment property, after deducting other expenses, is greater than the interest on the borrowings.

preservation age the minimum age at which a member can access their preserved benefits; a benefit may be paid earlier if the member has met a condition of release; the preservation age varies depending on when the member was born.

preserved benefits superannuation fund benefits that you can access when you reach your preservation age and retire.

private ruling written advice you receive from the ATO about how it would interpret the tax laws in respect of a specific issue you raise.

PSI personal services income — business income that is principally derived via the personal exertion of an individual and is subject to certain tests in order to be assessable in a company or trust.

put option the right, not the obligation, to sell underlying shares at an agreed price on or before the expiry date; a form of insurance in a falling market.

quantity surveyor a professional within the construction industry who is recognised by the ATO to have the appropriate construction costing skills to calculate the cost of items for the purposes of tax depreciation schedules.

reduced cost base the cost base of a CGT asset minus certain expenditure that had been allowed as a tax deduction; used to calculate a capital loss.

registered tax agent a person who is authorised to give you advice in respect of managing your tax affairs and can lodge a tax return on your behalf; the fee they charge for their services is ordinarily a tax-deductible expense.

reportable fringe benefits the grossed-up taxable value of certain fringe benefits provided to you on your payment summary.

reportable superannuation contributions the sum of any contributions that you make to your superannuation fund for which you can claim a deduction in the financial year under Subdivision 290-C of the *Income Tax Assessment Act 1997*, and the contributions your employer makes for you.

resident a person who normally resides in Australia; taxed on their worldwide income at the marginal tax rates.

Restart wage subsidy A program that pays employers up to $10 000 (GST inclusive) over two years who employ and retain eligible job seekers who are 50 years of age or older, and who have been unemployed and on income support for six months or more.

rights issue the right to buy additional shares direct from the company at a specified price (usually below market price) on a specified future date; usually linked to the number of shares you hold.

salary sacrifice a strategy where you ask your employer to put an additional amount of your pre-tax salary into super.

self-assessment   the tax system in Australia where the onus is on you to declare to the ATO the correct amount of income you derive each year and claim the correct amount of tax deductions.

sell contract note   the invoice you receive from a stockbroker at the time you sell your shares; it will summarise the details of the transaction and can be used to calculate a capital gain or capital loss for taxation purposes.

senior Australians   Anyone aged over 65.

senior and pensioner tax offset (SAPTO)   an effective tax-free threshold for eligible senior Australians of $33 044 for singles and $29 739 each for couples.

SFSS   student financial supplement scheme — a voluntary loan scheme to help tertiary students cover their expenses while studying.

SG   superannuation   guarantee — compulsory   super contributions paid every quarter by employers at a minimum of 9.50 per cent of employees' ordinary time earnings. Gradually increasing to 12 per cent by 2025–26.

shareholder   a person who owns shares in a company.

share investor   a person who invests in the sharemarket with the predominant purpose of deriving dividends and long-term capital growth.

share trader   a person who is carrying on a business trading in shares with the predominant purpose of making a profit.

SIS   *Superannuation Industry (Supervision) Act 1993.*

SMSF   self managed superannuation fund, also known as DIY super, a super fund that you manage yourself.

statutory method   method used to calculate FBT on company cars based on the total number of kilometres travelled and applying a statutory fraction to the cost of the car provided. See table 2.3 on p. 65.

super co-contribution   If you make personal contributions to your super and are otherwise eligible, the Federal Government will help boost your account with a super co-contribution of up to $500 per financial year; the amount of the co-contribution will depend on your total income level (you can earn less than $50 454) and the amount of personal contributions you make.

superannuation fund   A fund set up to finance retirement; benefits normally cannot be accessed until you reach your preservation age and retire from the workforce.

tax   Something we all hate paying and love to try and minimise...legally!

taxable income   The amount of income that's liable to tax; taxable income equals assessable income less allowable deductions.

tax-deferred scheme   Employee share schemes that allow you to defer paying tax; generally, you will pay tax on the discount you receive when you acquire ESS interests in the financial year in which you acquired them; however, in certain circumstances, you may defer paying the tax for a period of up to seven years.

tax-free threshold   The lowest tax bracket ($18 200) at which an Australian resident pays no tax; non-residents (including those on working holidays in Australia) cannot claim the tax-free threshold.

tax offset   A tax credit or rebate that you can use to reduce the amount of tax payable on taxable income you derive.

tax refund   Something we all love to get from the tax man each year.

tax ruling A public ruling issued by the ATO to explain and clarify how the Taxation Commissioner interprets tax legislation in respect of a specific issue.

tax man The nickname affectionately given to the Commissioner of Taxation and/or the Australian Taxation Office in general.

temporary budget repair levy 2 per cent levy introduced in the 2014–15 federal budget on the excess taxable income above $180 000 for three years from 1 July 2014.

TFN Tax file number — a unique number issued by the ATO to individuals and organisations to increase the efficiency in administering tax and other Federal Government systems.

TFN withholding Tax withheld at the highest marginal rate (47 per cent) on unfranked dividends and bank interest if you have not quoted your TFN; taxpayers need to include the amounts withheld in their tax return in order to receive the credit in their assessment.

total net investment loss The sum for the financial year of the amount by which the individual's:

▶ deductions from financial investments are greater than their income from those investments

▶ rental property deductions are greater than their rental property income.

Trade Support Loan A loan paid in instalments totalling up to $20 000 over four years to assist eligible apprentices with everyday costs while they complete their apprenticeship www.australianapprenticeships.gov.au.

trust A legal obligation binding a person (the trustee) who has control over the investment assets (for instance, a share portfolio) for the benefit of beneficiaries.

trustee The individual or entity that has the responsibility of ensuring that the trust or super fund is operated in accordance with its trust deed; trustees must also comply with relevant legislation and regulations.

TtR Transition to retirement—strategy available to those aged over 55 to access up to 10 per cent of their super each year tax-free to supplement their income.

under a legal disability A beneficiary of a trust, such as a minor, a bankrupt or an insane person, who is not in a legal position to deal with a trust distribution.

unfranked dividends Dividends paid by an Australian resident company from profits that have not had Australian company tax paid on them.

warrant An option issued that gives the holder the right, but not the obligation, to buy from the issuer or sell to the issuer underlying shares at an agreed price on or before the expiry date.

wash sale Selling shares to predominantly make a capital loss and gain a tax benefit, then buying the shares back immediately.

Bibliography

A New Tax System (Goods and Services Tax) Act 1999.

A New Tax System (Goods and Services Tax) Regulations 1999.

Australian Bureau of Statistics 2014, 5206.0 Australian National Accounts: National Income, Expenditure and Product: Table 30.

Australian Bureau of Statistics 2015, 5206.0 Australian National Accounts: National Income, Expenditure and Product: Table 3.

Australian Prudential Regulation Authority 2015a, Monthly Banking Statistics — December 2014.

Australian Prudential Regulation Authority 2015b, Quarterly Superannuation Performance — December 2014.

Australian Securities Exchange 2013, 2012 Australian Share Ownership Study.

Australian Securities Exchange 2015, Historical market statistics — December 2014.

Australian Taxation Office 2015, Self-managed super fund statistical report — December 2014.

Barkoczy, S 2015, *Core Tax Legislation & Study Guide*, 18th edn, CCH Australia, Sydney.

CCH Australia 2015, *Australian GST Legislation with Overview*, 18th edn, CCH Australia, Sydney.

CCH Australia 2015, *Australian Master Tax Guide*, 54th edn, CCH Australia, Sydney.

Fringe Benefits Tax Assessment Act 1986.

Income Tax Assessment Act 1936.

Income Tax Assessment Act 1997.

Income Tax Assessment Regulations 1997.

Income Tax Regulations 1936.

Raftery, AM 2014, The size, cost, asset allocation and audit attributes of Australian self-managed superannuation funds, thesis.

Sadiq, K, Pinto, D and Kendall, K 2013, *Fundamental Tax Legislation*, Thomson, Sydney.

Woellner, R, Barkoczy, S, Murphy, S, Evans, C & Pinto, D 2015, *Australian Taxation Law*, 25th edn, CCH Australia Limited, Sydney.

Index